The Western Scar

The Western Scar

The Theme of the Been-to
in West African Fiction

William Lawson

Ohio University Press

Athens, Ohio

Library of Congress Cataloging in Publication Data

Lawson, William, 1929-
    The western scar.

    Bibliography: p.
    Includes index.
    1. West African fiction—History and criticism. 2. Returned
students in literature. 3. Returned students—Africa, West.
I. Title. II. Title: Been-to in West African fiction.
PL8014.W37L3   809.3'9352   82-6372
ISBN 0-8214-0649-3   AACR2
ISBN 0-8214-0695-7 (pbk.)

For Pasquale Anania
and Robert Wolterbeek

Contents

Acknowledgments

Despite literary criticism's obvious and widespread fascination with itself in this quarter of the twentieth century, the proper study of literature is literature itself. Furthermore, any Western critic of the literature of Africa ultimately must seek his validation in Africa. Consequently, it is African novelists to whom I owe the greatest debt for the development of this study.

Chinua Achebe, T. M. Aluko, Cyprian Ekwensi, the late Camara Laye, Kole Omotoso, and Kalu Uka all received me graciously and encouraged my work, convincing me that this Westerner had seen something correctly of the nature of the literature of Africa. I am further indebted for information and encouragement to Eldred Jones of Fourah Bay College; Dapo Adelugba, Abiola Irele, Ayo Banjo, Omolara Leslie, and Ogun Ogunba of the University of Ibadan; Margaret Afolayan, S. A. Akundayo, and Richard Taylor of the University of Ife; M. Echeruo and Emanuel Obiechina of the University of Nigeria at Nsukka and Theo Vincent of the University of Nigeria at Lagos.

St. Clair Drake provided most helpful support and direction in my quest for funds to make my research possible.

I am indebted in many ways to William Chance for both years of unfailing friendship and kindness, and a fund of information.

I am grateful to Carl Rosberg for his extensive assistance in bringing this work to the attention of my publishers.

A model for any scholar, my wife, Kay, knows this process of intellectual production very well indeed. Her support is more than that of a loving wife and is all of that as well. My children, Kevin and Marta, generously relinquished innumerable hours, even weeks, of their rightful claims upon a father's time so that it might be a writer's time.

Chapter One

Introduction:
The Indigenous Stranger

Although both English and French African literatures grew exten-
sively in the 1950s, each had its true beginning earlier in the century.
Thomas Mofolo, a South African, had written a novel in his language,
Sesuto, as early as 1906. It was later translated into English, entitled *The
Traveller of the East*, and published in London in 1914. He wrote two
other novels, *Pitseng* (1910) and *Chaka* (1925). Two residents of what is
now Ghana also published early examples of African literature. E. Casely-
Hayford published a novel in 1911 which was later translated into En-
glish and published as *Ethiopia Unbound*. In 1943 a novel written in
English by R. E. Obeng, *Eighteenpence*, was published in London.[1] The
first French African novel, *Force, bonté*, by Bakary Dialbo of Senegal was
published in Paris in 1926. It was followed in 1935 by *Doguicimi* by Paul
Hazoumé, a Dahomean, and in 1948 by *Karim* by Ousman Socé, another
Senegalese.[2]

The steady move by African nations toward independence in the
fifties and early sixties was accompanied by rapid growth in the production of drama, poetry, and fiction. This literary flowering was largely
concentrated in West Africa, where several new nations were soon to
come into being. To a lesser extent, promising new works appeared in
South Africa and East Africa as well.

The Western Scar

In West Africa, Anglophone and Francophone writers of fiction dealt largely with nationalistic themes of anticolonialism and negritude, a philosophy that extolls blackness and African cultures. But one frequently recurrent theme, the life of the traveler returned from the West, illustrated another issue arising from Africa's colonial history. Just as African literature, itself deriving in part from European languages and traditions, occasioned questions about its basic identity, so too did the effect of Western education on Africans themselves. Many African intellectuals, whose Western educations may have begun in local mission schools and ended at Oxford, the Sorbonne, or Harvard, experienced serious crises of identity upon entry into adult life in their home countries. The crisis of reentry or, more precisely, the entire experience of the conflict between the individual's African and Western selves serves as a metaphor for Africa's still dynamic assimilation of Western cultures.

This theme is basic to the West African novel. In fact, Casely-Hayford's *Ethiopia Unbound*, the first West African novel, is also the first "been-to" novel. In the early 1950s the term *been-to* referred to persons who had been educated abroad. Initially they were looked upon with considerable respect and found easy access to prestigious, well-paying jobs. But many found themselves painfully committed to conflicting cultural values. This conflict of the been-to became a recognized cultural reality and, from the early fifties through the early seventies, a frequently repeated literary convention.[3]

Ethiopia Unbound tells the story of Kwamankra, a native of the Gold Coast (now Ghana) who has been educated in England. He has returned to his country committed to nationalism and racial consciousness. British officials and his fellow Africans are surprised by his attacks on colonialism and by his championing of African cultural values, a principle the author has named "Ethiopianism" (the same philosophy is to emerge twenty-five years later in France as *négritude*). Kwamankra's friends and the colonial officials alike warn him of the dangers of his outspokenness, but they cannot deter him. Unfortunately, the work is far from fully developed as a novel. The story line soon becomes subordinated to the exposition of Casely-Hayford's religious and nationalist philosophies. But the literary convention of the been-to is born in this novel, and its use has continued ever since.

In this convention the been-to is usually presented as having found his journey and his extended stay in the West psychologically disruptive. Marked in the eyes of his compatriots by his Western education and his long absence, he is involved in, not one, but two processes of adjustment: that of his return to his country, and all the complications therein, and that which traditionally follows formal education, the entry into adulthood. Even though his home in the traditional village may only have been lightly touched by encroaching modernity, he himself has undergone a transition at the center of his being. Novels featuring the been-to theme have often presented stereotyped situations, attitudes, and character types. Frequently employed, for instance, is a suggestion of the world as *The Waste Land*, that is, a tone of cool, superior irony, a sad view of the world. Yet the convention also requires that the protagonist, while external to his culture, be eager to enter the world at the same time that he holds back, consciously considering what lies before him. Affected by what he has experienced abroad, inexperienced in the complexities of the adult world (especially in the new Africa so unlike the traditional world he remembers), the been-to is drawn into a series of difficulties that lead even to disaster. While the been-to is at odds with the urban society to which he has returned, he also finds that the traditional society no longer works for him; he has outgrown its requirements. Consequently, one of his underlying problems is his isolation. The convention also includes the pattern of friends' and relatives' too great expectation of the returnee as well as commentary on the linking of business and political corruption at the expense of the general populace.

In various ways, some of West Africa's most prominent writers employ the theme of the been-to for profound social analysis. As the been-to discovers what has happened to his country since his departure, so the reader is brought to a greater understanding of that country's ills. The been-to typically is conscious of a massive breakdown of human institutions in his country. Bereft of the sustaining power of a felt moral universe, he sees how falsity and cynicism have replaced belief and commitment. He sees Westernization as a curse on his world. The been-to recognizes the West as a source of technological power and even, in some cases, of psychological power. But he also perceives it as devoid of spiritual value, as functioning in his community as an agent of disorder. The world is a wasteland. Images of excrement, symbolic of moral corruption, are not infrequent.

A general pattern, then, and a general weakness can be found in some contemporary West African novels: the been-to, bearing the Western scar of psychic division, fails to find himself in either of the two worlds that war for dominance over his sensibility. The weakness is that the characters often seem to be inadequately motivated and conform merely to the pattern rather than respond to some internal motivation or uniqueness of plot.

But the weaknesses of the theme should not obscure its power or its variety. Not all been-tos are heroes in anguish. Fat, expansive, success-ful, perhaps corrupt, certainly materialistic, Brempong of Armah's *Fragments* is a case in point. He illustrates the commonality of the type and at the same time suggests the enormous range of personality the convention can treat. Certainly, the convention offers as wide a range of possibilities as the Western tradition of the picaro, which produced such varying characters as Tom Jones and Don Quixote, or the theme of the young man from the provinces, which has spawned both Julian Sorel and Jay Gatsby.

It is the purpose of the present study to delineate an aspect of West African literary history from 1911 to the present. Although some critics have referred in passing to the frequent appearances of been-tos in the fiction of that period, no one has yet discussed the convention at length. I show that the convention, developing from cultural reality recognized in the early 1950s, rose fairly rapidly to a mature form in the 1960s, and in the early 1970s began to show definite signs of major new developments. Closely reflective of rapidly changing West African social conditions, the convention as it is now employed exhibits some changing attitudes to-ward the been-to. Change was clearly necessary for the continued life of the convention, for as O. R. Dathorne has written of the old standard pattern:

> The Old versus New School [the been-to theme] has become almost a kind of caricature of itself. It began perhaps as an offshoot of negritude and developed its own form and growth. Like all moulds, it has little room for inventiveness; it inhibits the individuality of the author and provides him with a ready made plot, wooden characters and a stage set environment.[4]

Several works wherein the convention is dominant will remain, however, universally significant literature, for the been-to symbolizes one contem-porary aspect of the universal human condition. The notion of the psychic scar that marks the wound of his division, his longing for a traditional pastoral haven in an idealized Africa on the one hand and his fascination for the freedom, challenge, and power possible in Western urban modernity on the other is widely appealing. For we are at once products of and participants in a similar revolutionary change of mode of life. Although that revolution has taken centuries in the West, many Africans experience the entire process in a single lifetime. In both cultures, however, the process causes members to long for the past at the same time that they look to the future. While the convention of the been-to provides a basis for commentary upon West African social conditions and a metaphor for Africa's relationships with the Western world, it also embodies the universal mysteries of human growth and decline. Because the developments of individual artists as well as that of a form must be accounted for, there can be only a general correspondence between development and chronology in this study. However, the pattern of rise and decline throughout the twenty-year period should become clear.

In chapter two, I discuss the emergence of the convention in Camara Laye's *The Dark Child* and Chinua Achebe's *No Longer at Ease*. *The Dark Child*, first published in French in 1954, is an autobiographical account of Laye's childhood. It foreshadows the been-to experience and at the same time shows one aspect of what lies at the heart of that experience. Laye has reported that the novel was written after he had been living in Paris for several years and feared the fading of both his childhood *and* his African memories. As we shall see, the emphasis is important. One of the central characteristics of the convention is the returnee's continual shock that Africa is not as he has fondly remembered it during his years abroad. *The Dark Child* is just such a memory.

The second novel to be considered, Chinua Achebe's *No Longer at Ease*, published in 1960, represents the classic expression of the been-to convention. All the basic elements of the pattern are included. The young man just returning to Nigeria from a successful academic career in London attempts to meet the conflicting demands of his twin roles as a son of a traditional tribesman and as a rising professional in the capital city of Lagos. Predictably, and conventionally, he fails at both attempts.

Chapter three discusses three novels that represent in varying ways the convention's most developed form. The first of these, paradoxically, does not employ the convention directly. Furthermore, it is one of the chronological anomalies. Nevertheless, Laye's second novel, *The Radiance of the King*, appropriately appears at this point in the present study, for it represents Laye's second stage of artistic development and therefore is part of the second phase of the convention as a whole. Although the protagonist is a European, not an African, his experience is an embellishment upon the been-to convention.

Cheikh Hamidou Kane's novel *Ambiguous Adventure*, first published in Paris as *L'aventure ambiguë* in 1963, is a lyric expression of the convention and reflects a mélange of African, Islamic, and French traditions. Out of Senegalese tribal particularities, Kane has created a poetic and mythic treatment of the theme, which approach contains none of the social realism of *No Longer at Ease*. Yet the two novels are concerned with the same issue and end without a resolution to the dilemma. Precise and subtle in its simplicity and depth, *Ambiguous Adventure* presents one of the most sophisticated treatments of the convention.

The third novel discussed in chapter three is the most overtly conscious treatment of the convention as myth. Ayi Kwei Armah's *Fragments*, published in 1969, contains many parallels to Achebe's *No Longer at Ease*. Yet Armah's protagonist understands and fears, considerably more than does Achebe's Obi Okonkwo, the psychic and spiritual implications of the Western journey.

The fourth chapter presents the decline of the old form of the convention and the beginnings of its new forms. Again we encounter chronological irregularity. Two of these works were published before Armah's *Fragments*, which might be considered the summit of the convention's development. Nonetheless, the flaws of these novels grow out of the fact that the convention had been in use for some time. Therefore, even though a better work was yet to come, they indicate the convention was in a decline. In these works the been-to's behavior seems to have been drawn from earlier models. Little individualized characterization or development of situation is revealed. Although not all the novels in this later group are failures, the far too familiar ring of the been-to's complaint strongly suggests that the convention has been heavily exploited. Wole Soyinka's novel *The Interpreters* (1965), an impressive work in many ways, is nonetheless excessively insistent. He gives us, not one, but six been-to protagonists. The basic elements of the story of each of them are already familiar. Laye's third novel, *A Dream of Africa* (1966), fails, not so much because he repeats the story now so familiar to the reader, but because the work tells almost no story at all. The elements of the convention swirl about the reader with almost no connecting links.

The chapter continues with a brief discussion of Kole Omotoso's 1971 novel *The Edifice* in which the been-to has a problem new to the convention, overassimilation in the new acquisitive culture rather than alienation from it. Finally, I shall discuss Ayi Kwei Armah's third novel, *Why Are We So Blest?* published in 1972. This latest expression of the been-to convention carries the theme to hyperbole. The excesses in this novel lie in the uses to which the convention is put. Although this novel is weak, its weakness in large measure owing to its employment of the convention, the novel also presents an important new attitude toward the been-to.

In the concluding chapter, I explore this idea further, discussing new forms of the convention and new themes that were appearing in the West African novel of the seventies. I also place this convention in the canon of the literature of Africa, account for its predominance and decline, and assess its contribution.

In spite of its limitations, the literature of the been-to tells a powerful truth, in fact, more than one. It is an incisive and moving form for distilling the historical essence of contemporary Africa. In the West, Africa remains little known. It has not yet become the tourist center that Europe now is for Americans, although its appeal is growing. Yet hundreds of millions of people are experiencing profound change unprecedented in their history. This process is, of itself, enormously significant. We are all going to be affected by it. In America a new Africa means a new perception of black people and hence of black history and, in turn, of American history and American reality. The heart of that change is recorded in West African fiction of the past twenty years and most explicitly through the been-to convention. The literature's immediate social meaning is only one of our interests, however, for it is an immensely wide-reaching literary convention. Even though the convention treats topical issues, a universal element of the broadest and deepest significance runs through it. The convention serves as an excellent device for inveighing against a multitude of forces we all experience: the chaos of changing environments and of social structures that are being erected at dizzying speed with little concern for the past, the age-old disparity between our ideals and our acts, our search for coherence, meaning, justice, love, beauty, and order. The been-to theme also attests to the freedom of city air and the true potential for self-actualization present in the technological world. Individual growth is thus balanced against communal needs. Although the aesthetic of the been-to theme grows out of a particular culture, it portrays very dramatically the late twentieth-century human condition. There are, furthermore, wide applications of this African aesthetic. As Samba Diallo, the protagonist in *Ambiguous Adventure*, says:

> Everything will depend on what will have happened to me by the time I reach the end of my studies. You know, the fate of us Negro students is a little like that of the courier. At the moment of leaving home, we do not know whether we shall ever return. . . . It may be that we shall be captured at the end of our itinerary, vanquished by our adventure itself. It suddenly occurs to us that all along our road we have not ceased to metamorphose ourselves and we see ourselves as other than what we were. Sometimes the metamorphosis is not ever finished. We have turned ourselves into hybrids, and there we are left. Then we hide ourselves, filled with shame.[5]

Baako, the protagonist in *Fragments*, sees something of the same fearful process at work but develops his insights a bit further. "The been-to," he writes in his journal,

> is a ghost in person returned to live among men, a powerful ghost understood to the extent that he behaves like a powerful ghost. . . . Maker, artist, but also maker, god. It is presumably a great enough thing for a man to rise to be an intermediary between other men and the gods. To think of being a maker oneself could be sheer unforgivable sin.[6]

At this level of meaning, the been-to takes on mythic properties. Ambiguity goes out of the adventure, and the stakes are even greater, indeed, very high. The been-to is engaged in trying the dimensions of the species. Where can we go? What can we do? What power can we exert over space and time and the forces of disorder and circumstance and still retain our humanness? Lillian Feder in *Ancient Myth and Modern Poetry* writes:

> A myth is a story which involves human limitations and superhuman strivings and accomplishments, which suggests through action, usually of a ceremonial or compulsive nature, man's attempts to express and thus control, his own anxiety about those features of his physiological and psychological make-up and his external environment which he cannot comprehend, accept, or master.[7]

Consider how many of the aspects of this definition are embraced by the been-to. His blackness produces predictable and unpredictable, but always deeply felt, reactions in the world of white racists. His identity and sanity are continually threatened. The external environment of his temporary world abroad is often hostile, menacing, and incomprehensible. When he returns to Africa, he sees that those same forces he hopes to have fled have preceded his arrival, and all around him, as well as within him, change erupts. It destroys the known, creating everywhere a frightening unknown and transforming almost everything formerly recognizable.

The pattern of the been-to convention is ritualistic in that it is a repeated ceremonial telling of a moral tale. Like all myths, it seeks the power that lies in knowing the limits. The impetus that gives rise to it must be something more than an urge to chronicle the topical facts of contemporary West Africa. Indeed, its origins seem to be those same depths of conflict and contradiction which have produced all myths.

As this study will attempt to show, the been-to convention's deepest significance for its readers comes through its particular Africanness but lies in its deep grammar, where its force asserts something fundamental about the nature of the human species.

Chapter Two

The Rise of the
Been-to Convention

Knowing the nature of the conflict of the been-to is essential to understanding the literary convention to which it is central. The African traveler to the West suffers more than the absence of friends and familiar surroundings. In the West, the sensitive African is aware of an intense disjunction between the culture of his home and that of his present surroundings. Indeed, his difficulty is not that he suddenly encounters a massive complex culture, having left behind a cultural void. On the contrary, the traditional African culture with its interwoven elements of pastoralism, communalism, ritual, and magic is also complex. And, at the same time, the African experiences the values and customs of his culture with great immediacy. The basis of the conflict is the seductiveness of each element. On the one hand, the West offers individual freedom, the power of intellectual tools, technological machinery, and material wealth. On the other hand, traditional Africa offers its peoples the peace of a known, coherent world, a felt moral universe wherein art, morality, spirituality, pragmatic acts, laws, and values are fused in the central concept of the communal life as the highest good.[1] The traveler's problem is not merely that the cultures are different. It is that they are, in many ways, in opposition to each other. So the been-to cannot simply bring his Western values as additions to those of his home culture. The aggressive, self-serving individualist, for example, cannot be an honorable son of his village if he refuses to pay for the schooling of a remotely related member of his extended family. Such conflicts between the requirements of Westernized life in developed Africa and communal life in traditional Africa are widespread.

It is this tension that is central to the convention. In examining Camara Laye's novel *The Dark Child*, a forerunner of the convention, and Chinua Achebe's *No Longer at Ease*, we shall see various facets of this seemingly unyielding opposition. This conflict is a fundamental characteristic of both novels although the tension informs the two works in very different ways.

The Dark Child:
An Archetypal Memory

Camara Laye's *The Dark Child*, first published in France in 1954, is an integral part of the been-to convention for two reasons: it was written in Paris after Laye had been out of Guinea for six years, and it recounts his childhood experiences with loving nostalgia. The been-to's fond memory of an Africa that-never-was is characteristic of the literary convention. The novel points to the issue of dual identities as the focus of the been-to's struggle. *The Dark Child* presents the struggle indirectly. One senses the force of a subtle determinism that leads toward the boy's departure from Africa for Paris. At the same time, the story carefully depicts these things of Africa that he deeply loves, his family and his home. The youthful protagonist is wholly African throughout the story; yet the novel as an artifact strongly suggests the author's personal division. Written in Paris in French for Western readers, *The Dark Child* is African only in part and yet is unquestionably so. At the same time, it is also clearly a French work. The book, then, is an embodiment of that process of historical change which includes the breaking and reforming of the shell of culture-bound identity—the central issue of the been-to convention. Before examining this novel in close detail, however, we will find it helpful to consider briefly Laye's first three novels.

The preoccupations of Camara Laye's first three novels reflect the importance of the theme of the been-to in West African literature. Each of these works, *The Dark Child*, *The Radiance of the King*, and *A Dream of Africa*, treats the subject of the private traumatization attendant upon the historical confrontation of African and Western cultures.

The Rise of the Been-to Convention

Appropriately, the child is nameless in Laye's first work. His is not only a private destiny; he embodies a major truth of midcentury African development. History has forced into being the moving scene of the boy's sad farewells from his family.

Camara Laye's third novel completes the story, bringing the protagonist back to confront his dreams and the cold realities of contemporary Guinean politics. Between these companion pieces, Laye's second novel, *The Radiance of the King*, seems to reflect an important aspect of Laye's Islamic upbringing, the notion that a phenomenon is made known by its opposite. Instead of an African's European education, the novel depicts a European's African education. Radically altered by his African experiences, the protagonist finds spiritual salvation as he is progressively disengaged from his Western sureties and arrogance and taught new respect for the philosophies and customs of the traditional African culture in which he finds himself. Finally, in naked humility he submits to the irrational uncertainties of fate. Whereas the first and third novels are closely autobiographical, this second takes up another concern. By presenting subtle details of African sensibility and spirituality, the novel gives us a view of the Africa that is most threatened by Western pragmatism and fragmenting abstraction. Therefore, Laye's first three novels, taken in order of their production, can be seen as a classic account of an African's mythic confrontation with the West, a historical encounter that often results on a private level in a need to redetermine one's identity and its defining contexts. For Camara Laye, these contexts are the holistic, deeply felt world he perceived as a child; the foreignness of Europe; the culture of Islam and its doctrine; and finally, the socio-political realities of Guinea in the early years of its independence. Laye's first three major works demonstrate, then, the recurrent preoccupation with varied facets of the been-to experience.

The Dark Child tells of the been-to's perceived past, or more specifically, Laye's own perception of his past. As such, the work can be seen both as an example in the convention of the been-to experience and as a document providing evidence of the nature of the experience.

For some time, the novel was considered simply the happy result of Laye's attempt to create an *aide-memoire*. In 1963 he said of the work:

Vivant à Paris, loin de ma Guinée, loin de mes parents et y vivant depuis des années dans un isolement rarement interrompu, je me suis transporté mille fois par la pensée dans mon pays, près des miens. . . . Et puis un jour j'ai pensé que ses souvenirs, qui à l'époque étaient dans toute leur fraicheur, pourraient, avec le temps, sinon s'effacer—comment pourraient ils s'effacer?—du moins s'affaiblir. Et j'ai commencé de les écrire. Je vivais seul, seul dans ma chambre d'étudiant pauvre, et j'écrivais: j'écrivais comme on rêve, je me souvenais; j'écrivais pour mon plaisir; et cétait un extraordinaire plaisir, un plaisir dont le coeur ne se laissait pas.[2]

"Living in Paris, far from my homeland Guinea, far from my parents, and for years in a rarely interrupted isolation, I transported myself by my imagination to my country to be near my relatives. Then, one day, I realized that these memories, then still fresh, could be, with the passage of time, if not erased, how could they be erased? Then, at least, weakened. And I began to write them down. I lived alone, alone in my room of an impoverished student and I wrote. I wrote as one dreams. I experienced my memories; I wrote for my pleasure, and it was an extraordinary pleasure, a pleasure which the heart would not let go."

The Dark Child is, then, a professed account of Laye's time-sifted memories of his childhood recalled by the special circumstances of his long stay abroad, "j'écrivais comme on rêve." There seems to be implied here an underlying fear of, or at least some discomfort at, the changes Laye felt occurring within himself. (This fear of metamorphosis is similar to that expressed by the character Samba Diallo in *Ambiguous Adventure*, as the first quotation in chapter one suggests.) The view of his memories of home while he is abroad precedes an insight into the real and imagined dangers of modern African mutability. It illuminates the traumatic experiences of been-tos in other West African novels.

In an interview with the author, however, Laye stated another reason for writing the novel.

Alors, donc, moi, je parle de cette expérience personnelle. Nous avons connu dans mon village les blancs à partir, n'est-ce pas, d'un endroit très éloigne. Je suis né, disons, dans un pays très petit . . . un village qui n'a pas cinq mille habitants . . . à peine. Dans ce village nous avions evidemment un précept blanc avec sa femme, mais que habitaient à sept ou huit kilometres de nous. Donc nous avons vécu de notre civilisation traditionnelle. Et c'est cette civilisation traditionnelle que j'essaie de montrer un peu, bien que j'étais jeune, je n'avais pas toute l'expérience, mais j'essaie de montrer la sensibilité et les rapports entre le père et la mère, entre l'enfant et son oncle. Il y a des raisons pourquoi je l'ai fait. Quand je suis arrivé à Paris j'avais dix-huit ans. Les français ne connaissaient pas très bien comment nous étions: est-ce qu'on avait des cheveux blancs comme eux, est-ce qu'on devenait chauve comme eu, est-ce que la couleur là est notre couleur, ou bien est-ce que nous sommes fades?[3]

The Rise of the Been-to Convention

"Well, then I'm speaking of this personal experience. We knew in my village white people at some distance, from a region quite removed. I was born let us say, in a very small country . . . in a village that had fewer than five thousand people . . . scarcely that—In this village, we had, of course, a white prefect with his wife, but who lived seven or eight kilometres from us. So we lived in the traditional manner of our civilization. And it was this traditional civilization that I tried to show a bit of. Certainly, I was young. I wasn't very experienced, but I tried to show the feelings and the attachment between the mother and the father, between the child and his uncle. There were reasons for my doing that. I was eighteen when I arrived at Paris. The French did not know very well what we were like. Would we become white-haired as they did? Is that color truly our color, or is it, in fact, that we have faded?

A wide interval separated these two statements, both made several years after the period to which they refer. Their contradiction provides some indication of what that experience was like for him. If both state-ments are accurate, as well they might be, in writing *The Dark Child* Laye sought two goals: to retain his Africanness and to be understood in Paris for what he was.

Although the novel was attacked for its lack of anticolonialism, critics who voiced this complaint missed a central impact of the autobio-graphical novel. As Janheinz Jahn wrote:

In *The Dark Child*, Camara Laye shows the new spirit of the French West African childhood not as something remote, primitive, something to be ashamed of. On the contrary: looking back on it from a distance, and having the technical skills European education had to offer, he discovered that these skills had been animated, and had been more closely related to man in his *native situation*.[4]

Laye's view of what his native situation had been reveals a seemingly self-contained, coherent society in a paradisical world. Each of the first eight chapters of the book focuses on some aspect of life in the region: the ancestral snake and a guiding spirit, the father making jewelry in his shop, a trip to the country, the rice harvest, the gift of magic, the village school, the night of Konden Diara, and the ritual of circumcision.[5]

Characterized by Laye's use of *we* and the present tense, these chapters evoke a strong sense of community and a long-enduring conven-tional pattern into which the boy is totally and unquestioningly assimi-lated. Laye's memory of the boy's felt commitment to and identification

15

with his world dramatizes the alienation the been-to traditionally experiences abroad and again upon his return to a changed homeland. According to Paul Edwards and Kenneth Ramchand, Laye's efforts to convey the sense of the boy's immersion in the life of his community makes *The Dark Child* an excessively sentimental work; that is, "to look at each of these chapters from the early part of the book is to see Laye at his best, but at the same time to trace the first fine cracks in the artifact."[6] However, what they consider Laye's excessive sentimentalism actually offers further insight into the been-to experience and, in turn, into the literary convention that depicts it. Edwards and Ramchand cite the second chapter to make their point. Let us consider it closely to examine their contention.

The chapter begins in the formless element of mud where, over a period of months, a village woman gathers tiny grains of gold to be made into a bracelet by the smith, the protagonist's father. The chapter serves as a paradigm to what would seem to be Laye's perception of what the expatriate loses. The process of the bracelet's creation, rather than mere commercial manufacture, is a long ritual act that includes the good offices of a praise-singer as go-between. The praise-singer flatters the smith to persuade him to put aside his other work in order to make the trinket. Once persuaded, the smith, as ceremoniously as a necromancer, smelts the gold and works the resultant wire into the bracelet. Laye clearly imposes the point of view of an older man's memories of the experience rather than create the illusion of a child's perception. Yet his memory entails unquestioning commitment.

> The craftsman who works in gold must first of all purify himself. That is, he must wash himself all over and, of course, abstain from all sexual commune during the whole time. Great respecter of ceremony as he was, it would have been impossible for my father to ignore these rules. Now I never saw him make these preparations. I saw him address himself to his work without any apparent preliminaries. From that moment, it was obvious that, forewarned in a dream by his black guiding spirit of the task which awaited him in the morning, my father must have prepared for it as soon as he arose, entering his workshop in a state of purity, his body smeared with the secret potions hidden in his numerous pots of magical substances; or perhaps he always came into his workshop in a state of ritual purity. I am not trying to make him out a better man that he was—he was a man and had his share of human frailties, but he was always uncompromising in his respect for ritual observance.[7]

As Edwards and Ramchand point out, the opening chapter, which begins with a reference to mud and ends with the completed artifact, achieves "mythic proportions, original creation of beauty and order out of chaos."[8] Additionally, the elements of magic and communalism are evoked. The village woman negotiates through the praise-singer, who thus acquires a function in the creative process, singing of the goldsmith's illustrious ancestors. The goldsmith's son and the apprentices are involved, crowding in to learn the craftsman's secrets. The boy knows of the secret purifying rituals of preparation his father must have undergone. Laye shows how the technical process of the jewelry making becomes communal drama.

> The goldsmith may be the protagonist, but upon him all eyes and hopes are focused: his success will gratify the craving of the woman, excite the mimetic imaginations of the apprentices and inspire the poetic skill of the praise-singer; it will vindicate the mastery of the goldsmith and be a token of the good will of the powers that be. At the end, the whole group is conscious of a task shared as well as a wonder achieved, and offer gifts and applause as the goldsmith celebrates with the great dance, the Douga, another universal expression of creative harmony.[9]

The sensibility of the author as a nostalgic older man is subtly felt throughout this passage. The holistic, ritualized interrelationship of people, time, and earth itself which contributes to the making of the bracelet provides a sharp contrast to the efficiency of Western manufacture.

Although Edwards and Ramchand criticize Laye's "inflated commentary" that "at its most amounts to a crude insistence on black mystery,"[10] they find more serious weaknesses in later chapters. In the chapters depicting the rice harvest, a disguised attack on Western civilization becomes more apparent. The authors quote the following passage as an example of excessive sentimentalism rather than mere nostalgia.

> Our husbandmen were singing, and as they sang, they reaped; they were singing in chorus, and reaping in unison: their voices and their gestures were all harmonious and in harmony; they were one!—united by the same task, united by the same song. They were bound to one another, united by the same soul: each and everyone was tasting the delight, savouring the common pleasure of accomplishing a common task.[11]

"If the passage," Edwards and Ramchand write,

strikes us as being too deeply rooted in stereotypes of innocence and happy peasantry in the tradition of the European noble savage, it is because Laye wishes to insinuate the same criticism of European civilization that Rous-seau and his followers made. But the trouble is not so much that Camara Laye should use these stereotypes, as that he fails to go very far beyond them. The cause of this failure lies, at least partly, in the author's concern to record the doctrine and no more, rather than to evoke a life in excess of the doctrine but in which that doctrine might be implicit.[12]

This might be a damning criticism of the novel if Edwards and Ramchand continued to record supportive evidence of their contention. However, they cite other examples of Laye's remembrances of childhood hardships as inconsistencies in a doctrinaire novel. They see his com-plaints of bullies at school and the cruelty of his guardian-uncle as having "no place either in his polemic intention or in the doctrine which the author feels it necessary to expound in the rice harvest episode and else-where."[13] Why Laye's honest presentation of unpleasant memories does not contribute to a balanced realistic account rather than an inconsistent polemic, the authors do not clarify. But their further charge is a more convincing one. Laye insists on the efficacy of magic in his father's powers as a smith and in his ability to communicate with a snake, itself sup-posedly magic, which he keeps in his compound; on his mother's ability to communicate with crocodiles and horses; and on the countryman's supe-rior abilities to perceive the occult properties of nature. While he reports on the deception of boys in the initiation rite of Konden Diara as a neces-sary fraud, he implies that his boyhood perception of magic in other mat-ters was correct.

> To what extent are we to trust his faith in miracles and countrymen's visions? Is it entirely honest of him to imply that the wicked West has emptied the haunted African air? . . . The loss of the "secret" in conse-quence, far from having anything to do with the opposition of country and city, Africa and Europe, is simply part of the process of growing up, in which the magic of innocence may very well vanish, perhaps to be replaced by another magic of experience.[14]

Yet this criticism suggests something of the nature of the formative qual-ity of the been-to experience which Laye permits us to view through both the novel and his account of its writing. *The Dark Child* was written while Laye was going through a difficult period in France. Its romanticized images of African life suggest that the lonely student shielded himself from the hardships of European realities by distorted memories of an idyllic homeland. These distortions reveal what Laye felt he was losing in the West—or perhaps wanted to feel he was losing. They tell us something of the character of the literary figure whose return to Africa is conventionally so difficult.

> And so, one day, I took a plane for France. Oh! it was a terrible parting. I do not like to think of it. I can still hear my mother wailing. I can still see my father, unable to hide his tears. I can still see my sisters, my brothers. . . . No I do not like to remember that parting. It was as if I were being torn apart. [Pp. 186–187]

Occurring near the end of the novel, this passage points to the mythic nature of the been-to experience. Leaving behind the intensely felt world of childhood, which has included a series of progressive separations—from village to town, from town to city—the young man now feels he is finally leaving behind something of himself, for now he will enter a completely different world where the very air will be unlike any that he has known. Laye wrote of that parting while he was still abroad and therefore evoked the scene with great intensity.

Even though the novel clarifies the been-to experience by showing its preamble, more importantly, *The Dark Child* shows how one particular been-to, at any rate, perceives his past. The novel itself, then, while one of many that treat the internal, private encounter with Western culture, also reflects one essential part of the forming sensibility of Camara Laye as he was deeply immersed in the difficulties of his long stay in Europe.

Logos in Lagos: *No Longer at Ease*
as an Ibo Cautionary Tale

"Books are not Life," D. H. Lawrence tells us. "They are only tremulations on the ether. But the novel as a tremulation can make the whole man alive tremble." That power to evoke a sympathetic vibration does not lie merely in the story, he is careful to point out, but occurs only when "a whole novel communicates itself," the whole that Lawrence perceives as "a strange assembly of apparently incongruous parts slipping past one another."[15] Similarly attesting to another aspect of the mysterious craft of fiction, Georg Lukács asserts that

> the realized intention of a novel need not coincide with the writer's conscious intention. It is the view of the world, the ideology or *Weltanschaung* underlying a writer's work that counts. And it is the writer's attempt to reproduce this view of the world which constitutes his "intention" and is the formative principle underlying the style of a given piece of writing. Looked at this way, style ceases to be a formalistic category. Rather, it is rooted in content; it is the specific form of a specific content. . . . Content determines form. But there is no content of which man himself is not the focal point. However various the *données* of literature (a particular experience, a didactic purpose), the basic question is and will remain, what is man?[16]

The two critical comments are complementary, Lukács citing the qualities of the novel as stimulus, Lawrence, those of its effects. Their combination suggests that a fully realized reading of the novel is an exact, and powerful, communication between the intuitive powers of author and reader.

Early readings of many African novels of the past twenty-five years often seemed to be limited to the sociological information they provided about newsworthy, exotic places. However, it is increasingly apparent that the true significance of many of them lies in the richness of the universally meaningful content of the novels, expressing the writers' intuitive responses to the world at large as well as to their immediate surroundings.[17]

Chinua Achebe is considered one of the leading, if not the leading, African writer. He has written four novels, each of which has often been read as an anthropological or sociological novel, if only because the works contained factual information that was often new to Western readers. But it is as literature, the whole novels communicating themselves to their readers' sensibilities, wherein the merits of Achebe's works really lie.

An emerging pattern in Achebe's four novels is his sense of the cultural trauma of Africa's still dynamic confrontation with Europe and America. In his first novel, *Things Fall Apart*, he tells of the destructive impact of the coming of British colonialism and of the inability of his protagonist Okonkwo to respond to the historical forces at work upon him and his society. His second novel, *No Longer at Ease*, extends the argument. Okonkwo's grandson is a young man of the 1950s, an early

Nigerian graduate of an English university. He falls into disgrace because his foreign education has penetrated his spirit and left him a divided man out of touch with the subtle but unyielding rhythms of traditional Nigeria. In his third novel, *Arrow of God*, Achebe returns to the historical setting of his first work, an Ibo village in Eastern Nigeria. The time is somewhat later than that of *Things Fall Apart*. But essentially it is still a period of initial cultural confrontation. His fourth novel, *A Man of the People*, was extremely topical, dealing with the political events of Nigeria of the 1960s. The novel ends with a military coup brought about to end the national disorders attendant upon the tumultuous political free-for-all in Nigeria's early years of independence. Published only nine days after the first military coup in Nigeria, the novel attests to Achebe's sound assessment of Nigerian social conditions. As Bernth Lindfors rightly argues, however, the fictional coup was not intended to be predictive of the actual coup. Rather, Achebe was making a satirical statement about the corruption and ineptitude in newly independent African states in general.[18] Moreover, throughout the novel an implicit indictment against the disruptive legacies of the departed colonial powers is evident—and his total works make another assertion, the imperative of dynamism. Those Africans who cannot grow as Africa changes suffer for their intransigence.

After several years of other projects, many occasioned by the Nigerian civil war of 1967–1970, Achebe is currently writing a fifth novel. One wonders if it will be another example of West African social and moral history.

In any case, one of his most successful novels has been *No Longer at Ease*, which combines a sense of Africa's history, the ancient history of the older traditions and the recent history of colonialism, with the realities of Nigeria of the fifties on the edge of independence. But the whole work is, as Lawrence says the novel should be, "a strange assembly of incongruous parts." Typically, the meaning of the protagonist's name, "the mind is at last at rest,"[19] is quite precisely at odds with the title. The ironic tension between these two elements is an example of a mood that characterizes the entire work. The experiential content of the work partakes of the tensions between old and new forces. In the tradition of the realistic novel, it presents the new, the contemporary social reality. Implicitly, it looks to the future, calling for change and adaptation to it. Facing the title page are these lines from the title's source, T. S. Eliot's "Journey of the Magi":

The Western Scar

> We returned to our places, these Kingdoms,
> But no longer at ease here, in the old dispensation,
> With an Alien people clutching their gods.
> I should be glad of another death.

In context, it is clear that the looked-for death is that of the old order in Nigeria, of those who cling to gods bereft of their powers. On another level of meaning, *No Longer at Ease* is an Ibo cautionary tale, the voice of the village elder saying, "These are the limits and those who transgress them are no longer of our people." On this level, the work is mythic, a conservative force that looks to the past and prescribes the known boundaries of human behavior. Obi Okonkwo's story is more than the report of a young man whose foreign education has unsettled his values and leads him, therefore, into trouble. His alienation at home is radical, for he has gone out of the familiar world and become a different thing. He is not contending merely with influential elders and unfamiliar ways of the new Nigeria. Having offended the gods, he is confronted with the force of Logos itself.

Let us consider these two significant levels of meaning that impart such power to the novel, the realistic and the mythic. In regard to the former, the story of Obi's failed assimilation into the life of the Nigerian professional class is an example of social realism that comments upon warring values of urban and rural West Africa. It presents an interesting characterization of the conscientious young man on the make. Obi fails not only because of his own youthful impetuousness and intemperance but also because of the conflicts between his newly acquired London values and the contradictory value systems of old and new Nigeria.[20] For example, there is no way that he can meet his parents' expectations. They ask that he meet his traditional familial obligations by paying for their support and for the schooling of his brother, John. At the same time, their pride demands that he live the expensive life of the successful Lagosan professional. His salary can meet the needs of one kind of life or the other. But his values, those learned in the village and those learned in the modern world, force him to try to meet the needs of both.

A central meaning of *No Longer at Ease* lies in the tension between two elements, the need for order and stability and the force of growth. The traditional society with its roots deep in Africa's history is the highest value of the tribal elders. They struggle to bring young Obi into line. Although he is extremely sensitive to their values, he is a product of his age and is as much formed by the West as by the old culture. A headstrong, imperfect idealist, he is also caught up in a relentlessly unfolding sequence of events which leaves him no time for reflection upon what is happening to him until it is too late.

Two forceful motivating agencies in the plot are closely linked, money and education. Obi's education, for which he has incurred a debt of eight hundred pounds, provides him with a well-paying job, which, in turn, requires an expensive lifestyle. His obligation is explained this way:

> Six or seven years ago Umuofians [the people of Obi's village] abroad had formed their Union with the aim of collecting money to send some of their brighter young men to study in England. They taxed themselves mercilessly. The first scholarship under this scheme was awarded to Obi Okonkwo, five years ago almost to the day. Although they called it a scholarship, it was to be repaid. In Obi's case it was worth eight hundred pounds, to be repaid within four years of his return. They wanted him to read law so that when he returned he would handle all their land cases against their neighbors. But when he got to England he read English; his self will was not new. The Union was angry, but in the end they let him alone. Although he would not be a lawyer, he would get a "European post" in the civil service. [Pp. 14–15]

The conflict between the opposing elements is joined very early. The successful student, a new Nigerian, is sent off to learn a new skill for handling a traditional tribal problem, contention over land. But Obi responds to values of the contemporary world at large. He is more powerfully directed by individual rather than communal motives even though his scholarship is inescapably a communal matter.

> The selection of the first candidate had not presented any difficulty to the Union. Obi was an obvious choice. At the age of twelve or thirteen he had passed his Standard Six examination at the top of the whole province. Then he had won a scholarship to one of the best secondary schools in Eastern Nigeria. At the end of five years he passed the Cambridge School Certificate with distinction in all eight subjects. He was in fact a village celebrity and his name was regularly invoked at the mission school where he had once been a pupil. (No one mentioned nowadays that he had once brought shame to the school by writing a letter to Adolf Hitler during the war. The headmaster at the time had pointed out, almost in tears, that he was a disgrace to the British Empire, and that if he had been older he would

surely have been sent to jail for the rest of his miserable life. He was only eleven then and so got off, with six strokes of the cane on his buttocks.) [P. 15]

With typical economy, Achebe combines in a single reference the bases of conflict. The unlimited academic success that is characteristic of the good boy and a startling poise and iconoclastic daring that lead to the letter to Hitler are the stuff of a legendary youth of promise. Surely what he will do will be out of the ordinary. Whether it leads to greatness or damnation, he is following the path of the elect youth of contemporary Nigeria. Education, still the privilege of a very small number of Nigerians, is a central concern of national life; the subject is frequently discussed in news articles—the opening of new universities, the expansion of existing campuses, the ongoing implementation of universal public education are frequent front-page items in Nigerian newspapers. University faculty, often highly respected, become public figures as the media disseminate these educators' pronouncements on various aspects of Nigerian life. Academic promise in the fifties, such as Obi exhibited, would have indeed stimulated a good deal of speculation and hope for the student's future and, along with these positive feelings, a good deal of burdensome responsibility for the student. For example, when he sees that despite such heavy communal trust Obi harbors a dangerous capacity for heterodoxy, the headmaster is brought close to tears.

Beyond Obi's course of study, Achebe presents almost nothing of the young man's stay in London. We are shown little more than his initial meeting with his mistress and his nostalgia for home, which homesickness occasions his writing a poem of an idealized Nigeria.

> How sweet it is to be beneath a tree
> At eventime and share the ecstacy
> Of jocund birds and flimsy butterflies;
> How sweet to leave our earthbound body in its mud,
> And rise toward the music of the spheres,
> Descending softly with the wind,
> And the tender glow of the fading sun. [P. 23]

The narrative states that "it wasn't about Lagos in particular, but Lagos was part of the Nigeria he had in mind" (ibid.). In this context, it is not immediately clear how the disembodied flight is particularly expressive of Nigeria, but after his return Obi recalls the poem with some bitterness as he looks at the rotting body of a dog in a Lagos storm drain. The memory of his nostalgia for Nigeria while he was in London intensifies the shock and disappointment inherent in any return to the world of fact.

Obi's disillusionment with Nigeria grows gradually. Despite some initial minor faux pas, he soon settles into what appears to be very promising circumstances. He has a prestigious and well-paying post as a senior civil servant on the Scholarship Board and an expensive car, and he is engaged to beautiful Clara Okeke, also a been-to, who has her own prestigious job as nurse.

Yet the minor false steps upon Obi's return signal more serious problems to come when his foreignness at home will be inarguably apparent. His dress and his speech are merely signs of the difficulties of Obi's reassimilation.

> Everybody was properly dressed in *aghada* or European suit except the guest of honor, who appeared in his shirtsleeves because of the heat. That was Obi's mistake number one. Everybody expected a young man from England to be impressively turned out. [P. 36]

He is introduced to a welcoming party by a pretentious secretary of the Progressive Union whose speech is full of rhetorical flourish.

> What a sharp young man their secretary was, all said. He deserved to go to England himself. He wrote the kind of English they admired, if not understood: the kind that filled the mouth like the proverbial dry meat.
> Obi's English on the other hand, was most unimpressive. He spoke "is" and "was". He told them about the value of education. . . . When he sat down the audience clapped from politeness. Mistake Number Two. [P. 37]

The minor flaws on the bright surface of Obi's promise increase even as his situation seems to grow brighter. The car proves to be more of an expense than Obi has anticipated. The repayment of his scholarship loan becomes burdensome. Furthermore, Clara tells him that she is an *osu*, a descendant of one who, along with all his descendants, has been set aside from the normal community in dedication to his god. She is another kind of alien in her own country. Even though Obi is a nominal Christian, Clara's announcement of her special state stuns him into a brief, telltale silence. Clara understands even better than he the limited extent to which Obi's Christianity and London education have freed him from the values of his tribe.

Because of the mounting expenses of his new life and his family's needs, Obi appeals to the Umuofia Progressive Union for a four-month extension on the date when he must begin repaying his scholarship loan. The president eventually grants his request but feels constrained to give some advice, saying, "You are very young, a child of yesterday. You know book. But book stands by itself and experience stands by itself, so I am not afraid to talk to you" (pp. 81–82). He reminds Obi of the society's purpose and warns him against Clara. "I have heard that you are moving around with a girl of doubtful ancestry, and even thinking of marrying her" (p. 82). Obi becomes furious and rushes from the room, vowing never to return. He rejects the four-month stay of repayment. "I shall start paying you back at the end of this month. Now, this minute!" (ibid.).

His actions are those of a young man freeing himself from his elders, clearly enough, but they are also those of the Westerner asserting his individuality against the communalism of the African extended family. The gesture is weak for two reasons: his insistence upon immediate repayment of the scholarship loans compounds his financial problems, but more importantly, the Umuofians' claims on him go far deeper than the matter of eight hundred pounds.

A direct correlative to Obi's insistent financial problems, another factor in the equation of life in Lagos, is the temptation to bribery. His position on the Scholarship Board gives him considerable influence in the selection of students for grants for overseas study—at least, so it seems. But pressed as he is with financial problems, Obi is a product of his Western education. He rejects an obliquely offered bribe from a man who seeks to secure a scholarship for his younger sister. Obi ruminates upon his resistance with some sense of accomplishment.

> After all, the temptation was not really overwhelming. But in all modesty one could not say it had been nonexistent. Obi was finding it more and more impossible to live on what was left of his forty-seven pounds ten after he had paid twenty to the Umuofia Progressive Union and sent ten to his parents. Even now he had no idea where John's school fees for next term would come from. No, one could not say he had no need of money. [P. 87]

Although the bribe has been rejected, Obi's purity is not fully intact.

Whether his thoughts are a careful weighing of the virtue of rejection or are a justification for acceptance of the next offer is ambiguous.

When the man's sister, an attractive young woman, appears at his flat, Obi's response, while nominally still correct, is considerably less self-righteous than his first rejection. When she is admitted to his apartment, Elsie Marks displays a precise understanding of the way things are done in Lagos. She is fully aware that her grade-one certificate alone is no guarantee that she will be granted a scholarship. Merit alone is no key to success.

> She avoided his eyes and her words came hesitantly. She was testing the slippery ground with one wary foot after another before committing her whole body. "I'm sorry my brother came to your office. I told him not to. . . . The most important thing," she said, "is to be sure that I am selected to appear before the Board."
>
> "Yes, but as I said, you stand as good a chance as anybody else."
>
> "But people with Grade One are sometimes left out in favor of those with Grade Two or even Three."
>
> . . . She must be about seventeen or eighteen. A mere girl, Obi thought. And already so wise in the ways of the world. . . .
>
> "Last year," she said suddenly, "none of the girls from school who got Grade One was given a scholarship."
>
> "Perhaps they didn't impress the Board."
>
> "It wasn't that. It was because they did not see the members at home."
>
> "So you intend to see the members?"
>
> "Yes." [Pp. 89, 90]

Although he is sensible of her attractions, Obi does not take advantage of her offer. But when he tells Clara the account of his surviving the twin temptations, she exhibits a sensitive moral acuity. " 'I think you were too severe on the man,' she said. . . . 'After all, offering money is not as bad as offering one's body. And yet you gave her a drink and a lift back to town.' She laughed. 'Na so this world be' " (p. 93).

But Obi was also meeting the responsibility of the host, a powerful social imperative in African cultures. As Elsie understands very well, visiting someone at home places matters on a different footing in a variety of ways. Moreover, Obi knows exactly what the situation is for young people in Nigeria who are after a university education.

And who could blame them? Certainly not Obi. It was sheer hyprocrisy to ask if a scholarship was as important as all that, or if a university education was worth it. Every Nigerian knew the answer. It was yes.

A University degree was the philosopher's stone. It transmuted a third class clerk on one hundred and fifty a year into a senior civil servant on five hundred and seventy, with a car and luxuriously furnished quarters at nominal rent. And the disparity in salary and amenities did not tell even half the story. To occupy a "European post" was second only to actually being a European. It raised a man from the masses to the elite whose small talk at cocktail parties was: "How's the car behaving?" [Pp. 90, 91]

In this passage, Achebe presents the heart of the novel's matter— metamorphosis. The process carries with it the absolute requirement to sustain the new role. Having, at great cost, become one of the elite, Obi is bound by its dictates. To answer the password question, "How's the car behaving?" with the admission that his car is not being used because he could not pay the insurance premiums or buy new tires would be unthinkably retrograde. Conversations would falter at the prospect of his shame (p. 96). The force of these circumstances carries Obi forward. Like Elsie Marks, who can see no alternative but to secure her scholarship with her body, Obi is in a position characteristic of the new Nigerian in which moral rectitude can become prohibitively costly.

The dilemma that Obi struggles against stems from his faltering moral courage and his inability to live up to his moral principles.[21] As events catch him up, his tragedy arises from his conviction that he must please everyone. He must sustain the role of member of the successful elite, the modern Lagosan professional, as unencumbered by tradition as the disembodied figure of the idealized Nigeria of his poem, supremely mobile in his Morris Oxford. But Obi is not free of Umuofia. He must pay for his parents' support; he must pay John's school fee; he must pay the Progressive Union. Far more confusing than the conflicting demands on his money are his own opposing perceptions of Clara. Obi of the world at large loves Clara as a beautiful and fashionable woman, whose values are very much like his own. But Obi Okonkwo of the village knows deep in his being that an *osu* is forbidden. The contradictory forces follow out their own logic. His debts mount. He borrows fifty pounds to pay his insurance bill; he owes five pounds seven and three for the electricity for his spacious apartment; he must renew his driver's license, four pounds for the quarter. The tires on his car are nearly worn out. Fifty pounds that Clara lends him to repay the bank is stolen from the glove compartment of his car. His mother and father, both gaining new power over him by their increasing frailty in their old age, show the extent to which they are Umuofians despite their Christianity. He must not marry the *osu*. If he insists, his mother tells him, he should wait until her own death, for otherwise she would kill herself. The roll of events does not stop. Irreconcilables force themselves upon him. He cannot marry Clara now. But Clara is pregnant. He can marry her or not marry her, but not both. Waiting is no alternative. His next step, to convince Clara of the need for an abortion, is no solution. Clara submits and, after a long convalescence from dangerous complications, leaves him forever. When Obi's mother dies shortly thereafter, he has lost two sustaining, if contradictory, moral forces. The anomy of Lagos claims him, and he falls into an almost unchecked moral decline that ends with his arrest for taking bribes.[22]

The swiftness of the denouement is aesthetically just. It is the logical result of the prolonged warfare that exhausts his spirit. In the end, it is the timing of the swing of his moral judgment that is ironically wrong, even as the historical timing of his whole life is wrong. He has just realized that a bribe of twenty pounds that lies on his table has sickened him beyond recovery. He knows he can stand no more of such a life.

> There was a knock at the door. He sprang to his feet, grabbed the money and ran towards his bedroom. A second knock caught him almost at the door of the bedroom and transfixed him there. Then he saw on the floor for the first time the hat which his visitor had forgotten, and he breathed a sigh of relief. He thrust the money in his pocket and went to the door and opened it. Two people entered—one was his recent visitor, the other a complete stranger. "Are you Mr. Okonkwo?" asked the stranger. Obi said yes in a voice he could hardly have recognized. The room began to swim round and round. The stranger was saying something, but it sounded distant—as things sound to a man in a fever. Then he searched Obi and found the marked notes. He began to say more things, invoking the name of the Queen. . . . Meanwhile the other man used the telephone outside Obi's door to summon a police van. [Pp. 158–159]

Even though Obi Okonkwo's court case would merge seamlessly into the reality of contemporary Nigerian life, the significance of *No Longer at Ease* is not limited to social realism. On the contrary, moving through the novel, sometimes overwhelmingly apparent, sometimes like a spirit not quite visible but always felt, is a strong sense of mythic import.

Speaking of the autobiographical aspects of *Heart of Darkness*, Joseph Conrad acknowledges that

> it is experience pushed a little (and only very little) beyond the actual facts of the case for the perfectly legitimate, I believe, purpose of bringing it home to the minds and bosoms of readers. There it was no longer a matter of sincere colouring. It was like another art all together. That sombre theme had to be given a sinister resonance, a tonality of its own, a continued vibration that . . . would hang in the air and dwell on the ear after the last note had been struck.[23]

Like many been-to novels that have followed it, *No Longer at Ease* is also a work of another art altogether.

Similarly, resonance, tonality, and vibration inform *No Longer at Ease* with much more meaningful implication than the topical matters of Lagos in the fifties. As I have quoted Lukács, "The novel's style is an integral aspect of its content and in this content the focal point is clearly man himself." In various ways, both deliberately and unconsciously (Achebe has acknowledged with some surprise), Achebe's style invests his protagonist with an aura of specialness. First, like the typical mythic hero, Obi has had an extraordinary childhood of legendary success and has exhibited outrageous daring in his letter to Hitler. His selection for study in England and his success there are also imbued with a special quality. It is vaguely suggested that there is something special about his identity and his relationship to time itself. Odogwu, an aging villager who functions as a ritual figure in Obi's homecoming, says of him:

> We have our faults, but we are not empty men who become white when they see white and black when we see black. . . . He is the grandson of Ogbuefi Okonkwo who faced the white man single handed and died in the fight. . . . Remark him. . . . He is Okonkwo *kpom-kwem*, exact, perfect. . . . As it was in the beginning so it will be in the end. That is what your religion tells us. [P. 56]

Later, when his mother has died and Obi has disgraced himself by his absence from her funeral, one of the Umuofians now living in Lagos says, "It is a strange and surprising thing, but I can tell you that I have seen it before. His father did it. . . . When this boy's father . . . heard of the death of his father he said that those who kill with the matchet must die by the matchet" (p. 150). He refers to old Okonkwo, whose story is told in *Things Fall Apart*, Achebe's first novel. Okonkwo, fearful of being thought weak, is compulsively aggressive. When a boy captured from another tribe is condemned to death, Okonkwo strikes first, even though, having raised the boy in his family, he has loved him like a son. When it is clear that the British colonial forces have conquered the tribe, Okonkwo decapitates their messenger and hangs himself in a cursed grove. Although Obi glows with pride to be likened to his famous grandfather, Odogwu's pronouncement carries a note of fatal prophecy.

In an interview, Achebe was quite specific about his meaning in this passage.

In a very real sense there's a line of continuation, of course, between a man and his grandson. In our [the Ibo] imagination, a man is reincarnated usually in one of his grandchildren. He cannot be reincarnated in one of his children, so there is a gap. I have a poem entitled "Generation Gap." I don't suppose that many people understand what it is saying. The idea is that in the imagination of our people, you skip one generation, the generation of your children and you can come again in your grandchildren. So there is usually greater rapport between a man and his grandchildren than with his children. You don't have the kind of conflict that you have between father and son. If you move one generation you find a lot of coming together again. A man is usually more at home with his grandchildren and our people say that this could be the man again. I mean he cannot be at war with himself. He is back again or he has the possibility of coming back again in this generation and so, when a man picks up his child and says, "My father," this is what he is saying, you see. "My father who is dead can come back." So the story is not just a kind of style of talking. This is the way it operates. And an old woman would call her grandson "My husband." This is exactly the same thing again. "My husband who is dead is back in my grandson and my grandchild." So it is in that sense that one of the elders again looking at Obi says, "This is Okonkwo exact." This is this man exact, so physically he looks like him, although in character Obi is a much milder person. This may be just the environment in which one grows up—that can turn you into either a very aggressive person, or a very mild person, but Obi is not as weak as some people make him. This is where the connection can be made, because he is very strong.[24]

Achebe agrees that Obi's strength to resist advice from his family and tribe is the main cause of his disaster. In this strength he is most like his grandfather. He seems to be a kind of ritualistic figure capable of transcending time so that in various generations he can embody the concept of individual sacrifice for the sake of communal growth.

Obi's mythic significance is especially clear in the context of his foreign education. Odogwu refers to Obi's education in England as "wrestling in the spirit world." The dramatic emphasis of the ensuing scene, briefly adumbrating the novel's theme of growth versus protective stasis, becomes centered on the conflict between traditionally animistic and Christian Umuofians. (In the passage, Christian practice is seen as one possible way of being Umuofian, not merely as foreign). A very important emotional tone is imparted to Obi's venture and to the nature of his return.

> The White man's country must be very distant, indeed, suggested one of the men. Everyone knew it was very distant, but they wanted to hear it again from the mouth of their young kinsman.
>
> "It is not something that can be told," said Obi. "It took the white man's ship sixteen days—four market weeks to do the journey. . . . Sometimes for a whole market week no land is to be seen. . . . No land in front, behind, to the right, and to the left. Only water."
>
> "Think of it," said the man to the others. "No land for one whole market week. In our folk stories a man gets to the land of the spirits when he has passed seven rivers, seven forests, and seven hills. Without doubt you have visited the land of the spirits."
>
> "Indeed you have, my child," said another old man. "Azik," he called. . . . "Bring us a Kola nut to break for this child's return." [P. 54]

Obi's father objects to the ceremony, saying,

> "This is a Christian house."
>
> "A Christian house where Kola is not eaten?" sneered the man.
>
> [Obi's father says] "Kola nut is eaten here . . . but not sacrificed to idols."
>
> [The old man responds] "Who talked about sacrifice? Here is a little child returned from wrestling in the spirit world and you sit there blabbing about Christian house and idols talking like a man whose palm wine has gone into his nose." [Ibid.]

The manner in which the old village men ruminate over the time-measured distance of Obi's trip suggests the passage's ritual significance. They give up trying to comprehend (in the terms of their own immediate experience) what has happened to the young man. They relegate the event to the unknown.[25] One interpretation, and an accurate one, is that the scene illustrates the dissimilarities between the simple villagers and the worldly young man. On the other hand, Obi knows their language and modes of perception because he was once one of them even though he will never again truly be a Umuofian. In this scene, the mythic character of the novel is clearly set forth.

Asked if he intended to suggest in this central scene that Obi is a realistic mythic hero who pits his whole person against the human limits, Achebe answered somewhat hesitantly. His response confirms Lukács's contention that the novel has the capacity to achieve its own intention, that is, that its final form may be quite unlike its original conception.

> I think you are onto something very interesting. It is a subject that I have not, in fact, myself, considered in this light. When the elder at Umuofia cites the rhetoric of the wrestler who goes to the land of the spirits, I meant him to mean it as praise. . . . For Obi and for the psychology of his people to wrestle in the land of the spirits is something forbidden. There is a cautionary tale about the wrestler who beat all his opponents in this world and then decided that he must go and wrestle in the land of the spirits. Of course, he comes to a sticky end. He is smashed by his *Chi*. And there is this conviction in the imagination of the people that there is a limit to man's aspirations and that this limit is set in this world. Ambition is not supposed to carry into the land of the spirits. It is only the man who is doomed to be destroyed that goes that far. This is the whole purpose of the story. Ibo people are very careful about limits to ambition. They are very ambitious people and therefore they are very careful to know how far a man may go. And there is this theme in *Arrow of God* for instance, there the story turns on ambition. There is this concern that a man may become too strong. So maybe, in a way, this old man was, in fact, responding to this kind of thing without being fully aware. I wasn't myself fully aware. I think when I wrote that, I was thinking purely in terms of a man who has done something great. One who has gone and wrestled the land of the spirits was a great man. But there's more to it, I think, if one goes back into the psychology of it. Well, what I was getting at is very difficult to put across, very difficult to put into words. What I was getting at is rather hard to explain. . . . In a way, he represents that kind of person. . . . In a way, I mean he is more and less; he is more than every man. [The Amherst interview]

The man who, for his excessive ambition, is destroyed by his *Chi*, that is, his personal god, illustrates very clearly that there are limitations to ambition. A sense of fatality hangs about the tale of the too-winning

33

wrestler; what is in store for him once he has passed the limits of this world is easily guessed. At the outset, a similar inevitability informs *No Longer at Ease*, which is essentially a long flashback. Obi has already been brought to trial. That in itself is the ultimate disaster for him, not the verdict. Achebe says that Obi has already tested the limits.

> Yes, I think so in a basic way, yes. The disgrace of his arrest is something that he himself cannot live with. For him, it is one of the most important things. He is a very sensitive man, basically a very good man. This kind of thing means so much to him. He is very well aware of what happened to him, even if he succeeds in getting out and even if he's successful on appeal. This is why I don't go into it, because all of that is unimportant, you see. It may be important to the people of his village, who are determined that he must not be disgraced, but as far as he is concerned, this is why I was intrigued you see, when you talked about limits. As far as he is concerned, he is really past the limits. He is no longer concerned. He can even smile when all of this is going on. It's as if he were looking at it from very far away. It's as if he were somebody who died, you know. As if he were some-one who has recently died and is standing apart and looking upon the mourners, perhaps, from the head of the coffin. He's not really concerned anymore with what's going on. [The Amherst interview]

The recounting of Obi's story, when his fate is known to the reader, is in a way the enactment of a known ceremony. Our interest is sustained by the immediate appeal of each phase of the story rather than by a suspenseful anticipation of the final outcome.

John Povey writes that Obi's downfall is "a response to a series of events too powerful to resist."[26] But Obi's character also shapes the course of his career. Even though the immutability of things powerfully deter-mines his turnings, the stamp of Obi's particular combination of strengths and weaknesses marks his path. The resonant language of the scene in which London and the spirit world are equated is intensified in the next scene. The old man mulls over one notion of the limits of things. Yet he participates in the Christianizing of an African tradition, an act that extends seemingly fixed limits.

> "Obi, show the Kola nut round," said his father. Obi had already stood up to do so, being the youngest man in the room. When everyone had seen he placed the saucer before Agbuefi Odogwu, who was the eldest. He was not a Christian, but he knew one or two things about Christianity. Like many others in Umuofia, he went to church once a year at harvest. His only

criticism of the Christian service was that the congregation was denied the right to reply to the sermon. One of the things he liked particularly and understood was: "As it was in the beginning is now and ever shall be, world without end."

"As a man comes into this world," he often said, "so will he go out of it. When a titled man dies, his anklets of title are cut so that he will return as he came. The Christians are right when they say that as it was in the beginning it will be in the end."

He took the saucer, drew up his knees together to form a table and placed the saucer there. He raised his two hands palms facing upwards and said: "Bless this Kola nut so that when we eat it, it will be good in our body in the name of Jesu Kristi. As it was in the beginning it will be at the end. Amen." Everyone replied Amen and cheered old Odogwu on his performance. [P. 55]

Logos is self-sustaining. When the normal order of things is disturbed, powerful forces move into action to bring them right again. This passage, even as it presents a ritual, is ritualistic in itself. Two opposing elements that would tend to disrupt the balance of things are fused into one. The wholly African ritual ceremony of the kola nut takes on the character of Holy Communion. Opposing elements fuse, achieving an equilibrium. Certain things can be done, certain others cannot. As it was in the beginning, so it shall be in the end.

So the issue is not one of opposing or rejecting syncretism as such. Some kinds of growth, or change, are possible. Symbolically, the old man, acting as kind of priest of syncretism, ritualizes that fact. There are other kinds of immutables. The novel does not say that the been-to experience is inadvisable, but there are certain cases, certain character types that can perceive too much or dare too much for their own immediate well-being. Achebe says:

Sometimes our own people say, "Are you suggesting, in fact, that there's no remedy, that this will happen to anyone who does these things?" Obviously not. There are many people who go to England and who come back well adjusted and successful. They don't run into any difficulty that anyone can see. But one takes a character who can make a dramatic kind of contribution to the argument, and this is not typical. This is not the Nigerian who goes abroad. This is not the African who goes abroad. It is a little worrying that they [many protagonists of West Africa novels] (and these are the most important cases) . . . all come to a sticky end. And we forget, in fact, that we suggest, without intending to, that there is, perhaps something that we cannot handle. I don't know that I would be prepared to go that far. Many people go through this and seem to come out unharmed. Sometimes it may even be that they are unaware of the problem. Having the kind of awareness and sensibility that Obi has can be a problem. Brempong [in Armah's *Fragments*] returns and is completely happy to be called a "white man."

Now there are people like that who don't know that anything is happening, you see. It's not that they are not well integrated, just that their personality is such that they don't question and go out to do battle with all kinds of things in their environment. So they are more or less blinded, you see. This may be a kind of advantage in certain situations if you are thinking of personal safety, perhaps. But a man like Obi cannot do that. He is too aware; he is too sensitive; he is too intelligent to go through life without asking, "Why is this happening, why is this so?" Joyce Cary has a phrase. He talked about his characters as "doomed to be free" and I thought that was a very strong and beautiful way of looking at this kind of person. He is seeking some kind of meaning of what freedom is, and we have to understand that. And if we are doing that, we're in for a lot of trouble and shock. This is why a lot of people like Obi are at once the kind of universal sort who goes through life wanting to know. Most people want to have a good time and go there and pick up their degree and practice their law, and have a lot of money, and there's no problem. . . . It is important [however] because it is people like [Obi] on whom we rely for an understanding of the world. We cannot rely on people who do not see anything. To understand the world it is people who go out and take risks and maybe are even destroyed, who tell us something. [The Amherst interview]

Achebe creates Obi Okonkwo, then, as a truly special man whose mythic role is to test limits and perhaps show the way to dramatic social and moral developments in his culture. But if lesser characters such as the self-satisfied Brempong in *Fragments* can voyage to England and return with his wealth to be admired by his friends and family for having become a "white man," what are the limits? Exactly what boundaries does Obi transgress that he should be brought to a bad end? Again, for this answer, we turn to the felt experience of the novel, Achebe's intuitive communication to his reader. As Adrian Roscoe writes, "The modern novel, partly because it is a written form . . . is not addressed to the group mind, [but] to the individual in the privacy of his mind and study; it comes from the pen of someone who is giving his own intensely private reading of life."[27]

Just as Obi's hunger for material goods or perhaps, more exactly, the entrapment inherent in his lifestyle, leads him to skirt the edges of a financial disaster, so a kind of psychic hunger drives him toward a moral disaster. Inevitably, he goes one step too far. This step is not the taking of bribes even though that kind of corruption is presented as an outgrowth of the metaphysical daring that is his real undoing.

Many been-to novels are autobiographical in greater or lesser degree. Achebe himself was not a true geographical been-to. But his education subjected him to many of the same kinds of tensions that the been-to experiences. He was one of the first graduates of what was then the University College of Ibadan.[28] Since the faculty was almost exclusively English, his schooling made him a kind of indigenous been-to. Achebe has stated that the conflicts inherent in a British education in Nigeria are dramatized in the novel (the Amherst interview). To point that out, however, is not to say that Obi's moral brinksmanship is the artistic embodiment of Achebe's doubts about the adaptation of a second culture. Nevertheless, like Obi, Achebe did experience considerable anxiety regarding his Western education. He has stated that

> some things I work in advance, but I don't remember working on this been-to idea specifically. It just seemed to me to come with the story itself, you know. Perhaps it was one way of dramatizing the kind of education I had, but to push it even farther away, to take it abroad. It may be that, because this is one of the central national issues, the hunger for an education. [The Amherst interview]

Asked if the kind of stress Obi experienced was common, Achebe responded, "Oh yes, oh yes, I think this whole generation feels this kind of stress. You don't have to go overseas, I think, but to bring it out most carefully, going overseas helps" (the Amherst interview). The mythic transgression that the been-to commits lies in the nature of his journey. An unthinking person like the materialistic Brempong does not travel the same journey that someone like Obi Okonkwo undertakes even though the two may sit side by side on an airplane. Brempong travels a physical distance, sees another culture's material wealth, and avails himself of it. He undergoes no change. An African materialist can remain himself in the West.

But Obi's is another kind of journey. For him, the West is in a real way the land of the spirits, for there he undertakes a venture as daring as that of wrestling with his *Chi*. He assaults the limits by attempting to become two unlike persons, an African and a Westerner. Brempong would never undertake such an adventure. But the child who wrote to

The Western Scar

Hitler has already exhibited that he has sufficient courage to confront demons. When he returns to Nigeria, Obi's two selves are at war within him. In attempting to be the composite of these two persons, he is a mythic hero struggling with the limits of human possibility.

Early in the novel, before his departure for England, he is given a kind of ritual warning about the importance of his choice of a wife. He is told by the pastor:

> "I have heard of young men from other towns who went to the white man's country, but instead of facing their studies they went after the sweet things of the flesh. Some of them even married white women." The crowd murmured its strong disapproval. "A man who does that is lost to his people. He is like rain wasted in the forest." [P. 18]

Obi heeds the explicit part of the warning, but he does not understand the implicit message of his importance to future generations of his tribe and the need, therefore, to marry correctly. (This passage cites his importance to generations to come. He can be seen both as the reincarnation of his grandfather and his people's past and as the progenitor of the future.) But even though his culture invests all young men like him with an extratemporal importance, Obi has wholeheartedly taken on a Western individualism; that individualism is made most dramatically apparent in his choice of mate.

Marriage is not seen in Africa as it is in the West, as an individualistic consummation of romantic love, but as a communal act, an alliance between two kinship groups for the purpose of procreation.[29] Although Obi and Clara both think they are free of their Ibo ancestors, they cannot simply marry. This contention is the major issue of the novel, the heart of the African/Western conflict Obi undergoes. His arrest and disgrace are simply the aftermath of the struggle.

Achebe has chosen an excellent device to give expression to a powerful conflict, one that troubles many Ibos.

> The *osu* people . . . form an element apart in Ibo society. They are people who themselves or their ancestors, have been bought and sacrificed as slaves to a deity of some kind who they thereafter serve. From that time onward it is strictly taboo . . . for them or their descendants to marry or have sexual intercourse with any free born Ibo. . . . Inter-marriage and sexual intercourse with an *osu* is not only [taboo] for a free born, but the idea of it fills him with horror. And this is true, though unofficially, of Christians as well as of pagans.[30]

38

So not only their marriage is proscribed, but even their affair itself. Neither Obi nor Clara is free from traditional attitudes. He demands that she explain her statement that they cannot marry.

> For answer she threw herself at him and began to weep violently on his shoulder. "What's the matter, Clara? Tell me." He was no longer unruffled. There was a hint of tears in his voice.
> "I am an *osu*," she wept. Silence. She stopped weeping and quietly disengaged herself from him. Still, he said nothing. "So you see we cannot get married," she said, quite firmly, almost gaily—a terrible kind of gaiety. Only the tears showed she had wept.
> "Nonsense," said Obi. He shouted it almost as if by shouting it now he could wipe away those seconds of silence, when everything had seemed to stop, waiting in vain for him to speak. [P. 71]

When he tells his old friend Joseph of his determination to marry Clara, Joseph says:

> "Look at me. . . . You know book, but this is no matter for book. Do you know what an *osu* is? But how can you know?" In that short question he said in effect that Obi's mission-house upbringing and his European education had made him a stranger in his country—the most painful thing one could say to Obi. [P. 72]

But Obi does understand indeed. He tells himself:

> It was scandalous that in the twentieth century a man could be barred from marrying a girl simply because her great-great-great-great grandfather had been dedicated to serve a god, thereby setting himself apart and turning his descendants into a forbidden caste to the end of time. Quite unbelievable. [Pp. 72, 73]

Here is an intellectual response. But his first reaction had been a stunned silence.

When Obi tells his father whom he will marry, the father's response is a strange laugh.

> It was the kind of laughter one sometimes heard from a masked ancestral spirit. He would salute you by name and ask you if you knew who he was. You would reply with one hand touching the ground, that you did not, that he was beyond human knowledge. Then he would laugh as if through a throat of metal. And the meaning of that laughter was clear: "I did not

really think you would know, you miserable human worm!" "You cannot marry the girl," he said simply. [P. 125]

The spirit world is evoked this time in Obi's perception of his father's reaction. This time Obi is not a stranger in his own country. He is very much the Umuofian for whom his father's response evokes a chilling meeting with an ancestral spirit.

But it is his mother's reaction that thoroughly undermines his spirit of rebellion. She tells Obi that she dreamed her bed and covers had been eaten by white termites.

> A strange feeling like cold dew descended on Obi's head. . . . " In the afternoon [she tells him] your father came in with a letter from Joseph to tell us that you were going to marry an *osu*. I saw the meaning of my death in the dream. . . . If you want to marry this girl, you must wait until I am no more. If God hears my prayers, you will not wait long." . . . Obi was terrified by the change that had come over her. She looked strange as if she had suddenly gone off her head.
>
> "Mother!" he called as if she were going away. . . .
>
> "But if you do the thing while I am alive, you will have my blood on your head, because I shall kill myself." [Pp. 128–129]

By varying their reactions as his characters learn of Clara's identity as an *osu*, Achebe achieves the effect of evoking the spirit world with notes of progressive intensity. This effect suggests Obi's mythic struggle. His own silence at Clara's announcement suggests the first stage of removal from the ordinary world. Later, Obi infers from Joseph's statement that he is a stranger in his own land. Then the presence of the spirit is chillingly evoked in his father's laughter. Finally, his mother tells of her portentous dream and, in an altered state, "as if . . . going away," she lays on Obi conditions that in impact are tantamount to a curse. In these scenes the presence of the world of spirits is suggested with growing intensity. Exuding other-reality, the interview between Obi and his mother represents the climax of Achebe's technique, dramatically fusing the realistic and symbolic elements of Obi's experience. The intensity of feelings that Obi and the others show reveals the power of the traditional culture.

At the same time, Obi's suggestion that Clara have an abortion demonstrates the extent to which he has been Westernized. Yet the grim details of Clara's abortion and her subsequent leaving of Obi make clear that both feel the act as unnatural and un-African, an act that defies the moral logic that is a keystone of a culture in which "to be an adult is above all to be married, to be a mother or a father."[31] In traditional African cultures, birth is not merely a single event to be recorded on a particular date.

> Society creates the child into a social being. . . . For it is the community which must protect the child, feed it, bring it up, educate it and in many other ways incorporate it into the wider community. Children are the buds of society. The birth of a child is, therefore, the concern not only of the parents but of many relatives, the living and the departed.[32]

During her pregnancy the mother-to-be is seen in a special light, for she carries a new member-to-come of the society. In many African cultures a marriage is not confirmed until the first pregnancy, so central to the culture is procreation. Barrenness is no mere personal tragedy for an African woman. Her case has much greater meaning, for "she has become the dead end of human life."[33]

In such a moral system, Obi's guilt about the abortion is heavy. Further, Achebe links it closely to the young man's guilt over his treatment of his mother. Thinking of her reaction to his pending marriage, he remembers the special bond between him and his mother.

> But when he was about ten something happened which gave it a concrete form in his young mind. He had a rusty razor blade with which he sharpened his pencil or sometimes cut up a grasshopper. One day he forgot this implement in his pocket and it cut his mother's hand very badly when she was washing his clothes on a stone in the stream. . . . For some reason or other whenever Obi thought affectionately of his mother, his mind went back to that shedding of her blood. It bound him very firmly to her. [P. 76]

When his mother dies, he is overcome, guilt-stricken that he has too little money to send home for her funeral. Though he weeps privately and cannot bear the thought of going home and not finding her there, he is conscious that he is publicly thought an ingrate. He consoles himself that he had done well to send all the money he could for the funeral rather than use it for train fare in order to be present. But the blood guilt is evoked again. "He washed his head and face and shaved with an old razor. Then he nearly burnt his mouth out by brushing his teeth with shaving cream which he mistook for toothpaste" (p. 151). At this point, he has

41

already lost Clara. She has submitted to the abortion but has left him forever. He has not married her, but he carries the guilt almost as if he had.

When old Odogwu says Obi has returned from wrestling in the land of the spirits, he is not really correct. Obi's mythic battle in the spirit world actually continues. It is the battle between two consciences in a single man. The ironic contrast between the novel's title and its protagonist's name suggests the novel's meaning. Obi would be a mind at last at rest and at the same time no longer at ease, in both cases because, to use a Nigerian expression, he has traveled. In London, the changing boy, sensing the process he was experiencing, longed for the Nigeria of his memory and wrote a poem idealizing "our noble fatherland" (p. 142). At home, surrounded by a series of disasters, he bitterly crumples a copy of the poem into a ball and throws it to the floor. During the two years between the writing and the despairing repudiation of the poem, he has indeed traveled. And, of course, the traveler is a basic literary convention because he dramatizes the fundamental literary theme of the bewildering complexities of growth. The traveler is an anomaly, a dynamic force in a stable society, at odds with the normal world, in pain because of the new vision his journeys have given him.

In Obi's case there have been no forerunners; he is the first of his small, tightly knit society sent out into the modern Western world. When he returns, "it is," as Achebe says,

> simply that the situation in which he has landed is not cohesive, and this is perhaps where the problem of the been-to comes in. He is not in a world that he can fully understand. In the time of Okonkwo, his grandfather, the world was fairly simple. You knew just what was right and what was wrong, what was admired, and what was not admired. It was a community civilization. It's a different thing today. . . . It's a different thing in the time of Obi, and this is part of his problem, and, of course, this is made much worse by his going so far away to get his education. So he is dealing with an impossible task. [The Amherst interview]

The historical problem of the been-to is no longer so acute. While still limited to very few, foreign travel is common enough to have become a fixed aspect of Nigerian life. Now traveling to the West is conventional, not extraordinary, behavior.

But the literary matter of *No Longer at Ease* is still a pertinent subject, for it is not only Nigerian but universal, not a matter of the fifties but of history. We always strive for cohesion and structure and reach out for some meaning that can be imposed upon the bewildering flow of experience. But the comforting order we struggle to create can destroy us by its very stability. So the presence of the questing figure who cannot find peace is vital.

Obi's story is a particularly focused form that in its entirety celebrates the wholeness, breadth, and depth of the experience of being alive. In that sense, *No Longer at Ease* occupies a central position in the tradition of the novel. For as D. H. Lawrence puts it, "To be alive, to be man alive, to be whole man alive: that is the point. And at its best, the novel, and the novel supremely, can help you."[34]

Chapter Three

The Maturity of the Been-to Convention

Obi Okonkwo did not say that he had wrestled in the land of the spirits. Odogwu, the village elder, had to say that for him. Obi is caught up in the rapidly paced events of his conscious life. He is only dimly aware of the mythic struggles within the shadow land of his unconscious. Obi's partial understanding reflects Achebe's only partial understanding of the ways in which his novel is analogous to the mythic Ibo tale of the over-ambitious wrestler. Two other novels provide this aspect of the been-to convention with a much clearer statement. Samba Diallo of Cheikh Hamidou Kane's *Ambiguous Adventure* and Baako of Ayi Kwei Armah's *Fragments* are clearly conscious of the scope and the dangers of their undertaking. In these novels, the been-to convention is carried forward to articulate expression of contemporary myth. Similarly, Camara Laye's second novel, *The Radiance of the King*, is another highly developed work that puts the been-to convention to uses far more profound than that of strict social commentary. Like *Ambiguous Adventure, The Radiance of the King* is a contemporary expression of African Islamic mysticism. The structured doctrine of Sufism strongly influences both works.

The Radiance of the King, published early in the recent history of African literature—1956—represents a sophisticated outgrowth of the been-to convention because it is the convention almost exactly reversed in that it presents the education of a European to the ways and values of traditional Africa.

The Radiance of the King:
A Sufi Path to Spiritual Coherence

Clarence, the dimly defined hero of the novel, is a European down on his luck in Africa. The education he endures and the spiritual salvation he eventually achieves provide us with a mirror view of the African's encounter with Europe. This may not have been Camara Laye's intention, but in the context of West African fiction of the past twenty years, it is an inescapable effect. What Clarence struggles to acquire, an African sensibility, his African counterpart in Europe is in danger of losing. What Clarence finally struggles free of—his Westernness—the African, often at too great a price, works diligently to acquire. An analysis of *The Radiance of the King*, then, can aid our understanding of the been-to convention.

One reading of the novel could make it a satire of Africa's eager repudiation of its cultural subtleties in exchange for Western skills and goods. A more direct interpretation of the work would suggest a defense of the African cultures, particularly as manifest through Islamic sensibility. The conflict in *The Radiance of the King* is as much between Islamic spirituality and Western pragmatism as it is between Europe and Africa.[1] The alembic of Clarence's transformation is not merely an exchange of his European ways for African traits; it is a journey to God through successive preparatory stages very closely resembling the Sufi Path that leads to salvation, an aspect of the Islamic tradition. Rather than simply replace one adaptation for another, Clarence develops and thereby comes to greater self-knowledge by confronting his limitations, from which he had been shielded by his European perceptions. After he has undergone a series of confusing experiences that teach him the inapplicability of his European notions, he begins to change and to undergo the stages of development which make up the Sufi Path to God: repentance, abstinence, renunciation, poverty, patience, trust in God, and satisfaction. Also associated with the stages, "the ascetic and ethical discipline of the Sufi," are the states "which form a similar psychological chain." These are ten: meditation, nearness to God, love, fear, hope, longing, intimacy, tranquility, contemplation, and certainty. The Path of the Sufi ends only when one has passed through all stages. One does not move to the next until he has achieved perfection in his present stage. In any of these he may experience any one of the states that God decides he will endure. In the end, he is raised to a permanent state on the higher planes of consciousness, the gnosis. Then the seeker has become a knower or gnostic and "realizes that knowledge, knower, and known are One."[2] Tracing Clarence's African adventure, we shall see how in a general way he follows the Sufi Path to salvation.

That Clarence's adventure is to be one of radical psychological and spiritual transformation is made clear almost from the outset of the novel. Laye demonstrates early on that Clarence has stepped into a world that requires a different kind of vision for making one's way. This is a very distant Africa. Clarence slowly learns the ineffectiveness of Europe's tools of rationalism to deal with the issues that he faces in this very unfamiliar place. *The Radiance of the King*, like *Alice in Wonderland*, undermines some of our most unquestioned beliefs.

Clarence's original purpose is simply to solve his financial problem by service to the King by, in some vague way, capitalizing on his whiteness. " 'I'm not "just anybody",' he announces, 'I'm a white man.' "[3] But his first view of the King alters his course. The King's features remind him of "an inner life . . . but—what sort of inner life? Perhaps of the very life which lies beyond death. . . . 'Can that be the sort of life I have come here to find?' wondered Clarence. . . . 'What kind of life could it be?' he asked himself. A sort of abyss opened up under his feet as he thought about it" (p. 34).

With the help of a proud and knowing beggar and two confusingly similar boys, Nagoa and Noaga, he will make his way south for another attempt at an audience. But already he has seen that a meeting with the King will have a much deeper meaning than he had at first expected. Although he does not yet know it, Clarence is about to embark upon a quest for salvation, a quest that will undermine many of his Western illusions. One of the first of his convictions to be called into question is the most basic and all-encompassing, his conviction that reality is exactly as he perceives it. Even his identity becomes uncertain. " 'Am I not a white man?' cried Clarence" (p. 24).

There is something dubious in this matter, for white men do not come to the esplanade, where, hot and dusty, Clarence awaits the King.

The man to whom he speaks makes as if to spit, clearly indicating his contempt; if indeed Clarence is white, that color carries no special significance for this man. Clarence begins to see himself in an entirely new light. The spiritual journey will teach him other new truths as well. When the beggar promises to put in a good word for him with the King, Clarence is aghast at his presumption; but he learns that in the spiritual world of traditional Africa, the beggar's calling is prestigious, and he can be helpful indeed. After his initial annoyance, Clarence decides to accept the beggar's help. After all, he seems to know his way about, and Clarence's circumstances are less than the best. In this initial encounter, Clarence's pride is somewhat diminished. He is capable of a more realistic assessment of his situation. He is in another world; different systems of value prevail here. A beggar in the world of Islam is highly respected as a truly spiritual person.

> True poverty is not merely a lack of wealth but a lack of desire for wealth
> . . . the "poor man" (*faqir*) and the mendicant are names by which the
> Mohammedan Mystic is proud to be known, because they imply that he is
> to be stripped of every thought or wish that would divert his mind from
> God.[4]

So, despite what seems apparent to Western eyes to be the contrary, Clarence is fortunate in his guide. His perceptions begin to alter.

But his pride and his conviction of the truth of his perceptions still must undergo considerably more refinement before Clarence is worthy of the regard of the King. The process of his refinement leads him to such encounters with legal systems that his certitude of what justice is is undermined. He also finds himself in recurring dreamlike labyrinths where he is either the pursued or the pursuer. His certitude of reality is shaken, for he is no longer certain whether he is awake or dreaming. (In fact, he often sleeps a good deal or is very drowsy. This is another Sufism. The sinner is frequently likened to one who is asleep. Similarly, repentance is likened to the soul's awakening.)[5]

The south, where Clarence will again seek an audience with the King, is more than a simple metaphor for an Islamic tenet. As James Olney asserts, the setting itself is a major source of Clarence's moral and physical development.

> It is an exact and felicitous stroke to characterize "the South" as a place, or a
> state of being, where both body and spirit are nourished by the senses, a

place where both are bathed in a constant sensory flow, for it is the fantastic, overwhelming richness of sensory experiences that first strikes the visitor to Africa, especially West Africa (for example, Clarence) and comes to stand in his mind for the experience of Africa herself: the calls of strange birds, the chattering of monkeys, the unidentifiable cries of unidentifiable animals in the night, and the sounds of drums and men's voices when the moon is full, carrying so far and seeming to mean something so mysterious; the smell of dried fish and palm oil, the smell of coffee-blossoms and orange-blossoms, so sweet, so pervasive, so insidious it finally, as if from within, drowns the sense of smell; the taste of cayenne pepper and the taste of palm oil and palm wine and palm butter and of the marvellously named butter pear; the taste of pineapples, oranges, limes, bananas; the red-brown earth and the intensely green forest; the sharp, almost painful yellow-white of the moon in dry season, the apocalyptic colors of sunset; the purple-black skins of the people and the brilliant indigoes, whites, greens, reds of women's garments in Dakar; the moisture of the atmosphere that surrounds and embraces one like a damp cloth, a flannel that touches the skin at every point and gives a sense of pressure, of resistance to movement in the circumambient air. Immersed in this amniotic, total experience of the senses, Clarence is reborn at the end of the novel into a new and integral existence.[6]

In the village of Aziana where he will await the King, Clarence is sold, without his knowledge, by the beggar for a wife and a mule. The intoxicating odors of the tropical vegetation blind him to the truth of the nature of his service, stud to the harem of the Naba, a local high dignitary. Drugged by the tropical perfume, he does not realize that he makes love with a different woman each night. Only long after, when he realizes that the many mulatto children in the Naba's harem are his own, does he understand the slighting references to him as a "fighting cock."

One of the phases of Clarence's moral development involves his notions of luck, or the will of God. As the novel begins, his luck has failed him; he has lost all his money at cards. Yet, in his vague notion that an audience with the King will somehow serve him well, he again counts on fortune to come to his aid.

Near the novel's end, however, he says bitterly, "Luck! . . . If I had the heart to laugh, I would split my sides . . . Luck . . . . " He is interrupted by the fat master of the harem, Samba Baloum.

> "Call it whatever you like that's the name I give it. Perhaps it doesn't mean anything; and perhaps it means a great deal. Who can tell?

All I know is—and I'm absolutely sure of this—that if it exists, it won't be handed to you on a silver platter. He who expects nothing must not be surprised if he comes back with empty hands. And finally if no one is favoured all the time, no one is frustrated all the time. Luck . . . You see now what I mean . . . and what others mean when they talk of 'merit.' "

"The beggar used to call it 'favour,' " [says another.]

"I call it 'pity,' " [Diallo adds.]

"Give it whatever name you like," said Samba Baloum. . . . "allow me to call it 'luck.' But bumpkin that I am, I am not so rustic that I believe that this 'luck' comes only to the cleverest person. . . . I believe even less that it [has] something to do with the words 'right' and 'just.' Clarence . . . [t]hat is why I am telling you to seize your chance, for it is in your reach; . . . for if you don't make the effort you will never do it." [Pp. 247–248]

The harem master's advice is an important phase of Clarence's education. He slowly comes to understand how important it is that whatever the nature of the world, however uncertain fate and the human will may be, one must live up to his responsibilities to achieve spiritual salvation.

Then, finally, when he understands his moral baseness and his self-delusion, he is fully embarked on the Sufi way, repenting, abstaining from, and renouncing his sexuality and pride. Having long abandoned his interest in wealth, he achieves patience, trust in God, and when the King finally arrives in Aziana, acquiesence in the will of God.

Having seen himself clearly, Clarence falls into despair at the sight of the King's splendor. The very image of that which he has so long sought and awaited prevents Clarence's moving to him.

For the more Clarence looked at the King the more he realized what courage . . . would be needed to go up to him.

And it was not just his nakedness, it was not just his vileness which prevented Clarence from going up to him; it was something else—many other things. It was . . . the same adorable fragility, the same formidable strength . . . ; the same far off smile which like the look in his eyes could be taken for disdain . . . and which seemed to float about his lips rather than be an actual part of them. And probably his garments, too—the immaculate whiteness of the mantle, the gold of the twisted rope tied like a heavy turban around his head; so many other things too . . . that would have taken a lifetime to enumerate. . . . But above all, so much purity, so much blazing purity. All these prevented Clarence from going up to him. "Those are the things I am losing forever . . . ," said Clarence. [P. 250]

The Maturity of the Been-to Convention

At this point, the state of longing, which was bestowed on him at the outset of the story when he first sees the King, is most acute. He longs to go back and relive his life. A thought sustains him.

> And yet . . . my good-will . . . he thought. It's not true that I was lacking in good-will. . . . I was weak, no one has ever been as weak as I am; and at nights I was like a lustful beast. . . . Yet I did not enjoy my weakness, I did not love the beast that was inside me; I should have liked to throw off that weakness and I should have liked not to be that beast. . . . No, it's not true that I was lacking in good-will. . . . But of what use was this good-will? Clarence was about to curse it, curse it for its failure to help him and the tears sprang to his eyes. But at that very moment the King turned his head, turned it imperceptibly and his glance fell upon Clarence. That look was neither cold, nor hostile. That look . . . did it not seem to call to him? [P. 251]

Clarence's self-effacement is tempered by his understanding of the basic virtue of his good-will. At this moment, his clear understanding of the two sides of his being, his human weakness and his aspiration toward the good, is the highest point he has reached on the Sufi Path. It has earned him the King's steady attention, *le regard du roi*. ("The radiance of the king," which shifts the focus of the novel's meaning somewhat, is a poor translation of the French title.)

> That look still did not turn away from him. "My Lord! My Lord!" Clarence kept whispering, is it true that you were calling me? Is it true that the odour which is upon me does not offend you and does not make you turn away in horror? . . . .
> "Did you not know that I was waiting for you?" asked the King.
> And Clarence placed his lips upon the faint and yet tremendous beating of that heart. Then the King slowly closed his arms around him, and his great mantle swept about him and enveloped him forever. [Pp. 252–253]

At the culminating moment of his African education, he has purged himself of old illusions, renounced his sins, and achieved salvation. Like the African who journeys north, Clarence has undergone a mythic journey to the defining edges of his being. However, unlike the traveling African whose journey often produces fragmentation and madness, Clarence has achieved wholeness. He has seen both his bestial and his spiritual selves and has cast off his animal nature.

Laye's technique of undermining the expectations of the reader and the vaguely threatening labyrinthine settings of the novel have been called Kafkaesque. Eustace Palmer attributes other aspects of *The Radiance of the King* to Kafka's influence: the theme of the quest, Clarence's isolation and bewilderment, his featurelessness and helplessness, and the recurrent images of corridors.[7] Surely Kafka's influence upon Laye is important. Laye has commented on his view of Kafka's work. Having read his biography and his works, Laye concluded that Kafka's technique was also an African technique.

Il m'a semblé que sa technique de roman, qu'on appelle la technique de Kafka, n'était pas la technique de Kafka; c'était la technique africaine. C'est une technique typiquement africaine. Ce qu'il y a africaine, c'est le systême de rêves. Par example, si vous allez dans un village, si vous assistez à un conte, on vous dira, je vous raconte un événement. Cet événement s'est passé quand je portais ma mère dans le dos, et quand j'avais mon père à mes pieds. Donc, ça devient du Kafka, mais plus que de Kafka. Ça veut dire que cet événement est un événement imaginé; c'est un événement révé . . . plus que l'imagination.

Alors . . . quand j'ai écrit ce roman, je parlais alors de l'expérience spirituelle d'un blanc qui débarque en Afrique. Alors, beaucoup de monde a dit c'est du Kafka, et tout ça.

C'est pas Kafka. C'est la technique qui est kafkaënne, mais l'esprit est africain. Je pense que Kafka est gris. Il n'y a pas d'espoir . . . Ses héros n'ont pas d'espoir. Mais en Afrique il y a toujours de l'espoir. Et dans ce roman le blanc dont il est question et qui était en quête de Dieu, a trouvé Dieu.[8]

"It seemed to me that what we call his technique of the novel, what one calls Kafka's technique, was not [his]. It was the African technique. It was a typically African technique. That which is typically African is the system of dreams. For example, if you go into a village, if you attend a story telling, someone will say to you, 'I'm going to tell you of an event. This event occurred when I used to carry my mother around on my back and when I used to have my father at my feet.' That, then, became something of Kafka but more than Kafka. That means that this event is an imagined event; it is a dreamed event, more than [something of] the imagination. Then . . . when I wrote the novel I was speaking then of the spiritual adventure of a white man who lands in Africa. Many people said, "This is from Kafka, and all that. It's not Kafka. It is the technique that is Kafkaesque, but the spirit is African. I think Kafka is grey. There is no hope there. His heroes have no hope. But there is always hope in Africa. And in this novel the white protagonist who was in search of God found Him."

Laye concurred that Clarence follows the Sufi Path to salvation, adding, "Mais avec Kafka il n'allait pas trouver Dieu." Kafka's work attracted him, Laye stated, because of its similarity to works from African oral traditions. Both, he believes, derive from some universal archetype.

> Moi, je remarque, c'est une remarque, que les techniques dans le roman sont les mêmes. Il y a trois ou quatres techniques. On est obligé d'adopter ces techniques universelles. Et il m'a semblé que la technique de Kafka, appellée de Kafka, bien sûr,—les africains avaient avant des colons, quoi, avant des français, des portuguais, et des anglais. Mais ils, n'avaient pas d'ecriture, donc on ne peut pas connaître leur technique. [The Dakar interview]
>
> "I have noticed, it is just a remark, that the techniques of the novel are the same. There are three or four techniques. One is obliged to adopt these universal techniques. It seems to me that the Kafka technique, that which is *called* the Kafka technique, Africans had before the colonials, that is before the French, the Portuguese and the English. But they did not have writing, so their technique could not be known."

Although one must always exercise some caution regarding a novelist's pronouncements about his own works, these comments suggest that Laye's conscious indebtedness to Kafka is somewhat less than earlier supposed. One must guard against the practice of seeking European origins for those African things he admires.

On the other hand, one must be careful not to see *The Radiance of the King* as more original than it actually is. Eustace Palmer has praised it for its "clean break from stock themes: the clash between old and the new, the decay of traditional values and the evils of colonialism." He writes further, "Signs of such maturity have appeared only recently, but Camara Laye pointed the way as early as 1956. . . . Laye's novel can properly be described as metaphysical rather than sociological."[9]

This reversal of the been-to theme is important to this study and not only for its adumbration of those sensibilities that are threatened when an African studies in the West. The work also suggests a good deal about Camara Laye, who might well be considered an archetypal been-to. Very possibly the work reflects quite directly the longing and doubts that Laye was continuing to experience during his protracted stay in Paris. He may indeed have felt a need for the kind of purgation of Western perceptions that Clarence undergoes. *The Radiance of the King* is also a remarkable companion piece to *Ambiguous Adventure*, which we shall examine next. While Clarence achieves a spiritual wholeness in Africa, Samba Diallo of *Ambiguous Adventure* suffers a fatal spiritual division in Europe. Clearly, both novels represent a response to the same psychological phenomenon.

Even though the maturity and the metaphysical quality of *The Radiance of the King* are unquestioned, the nature of its maturity should be considered closely. The stock themes, then, are surely here, but not as objects of central focus. Rather, the clash between old and new, the danger to the old values, and the colonial burden upon Africa are omnipresent throughout the novel. Camara Laye's artistic achievement, the maturity apparent in the work, is the form of their presentation. Clarence is the West; the King is Africa, the embodiment of its traditional ways which are so threatened by the accelerated encroachment of Western technology.

What Clarence finds so difficult to achieve, sensitive Africans, been-tos or not, struggle to retain. The novel is indeed metaphysical, not sociological. It is also an expression of a heartfelt wish for the survival of something of the endangered cultures—or perhaps a gesture of farewell.

Ambiguous Adventure:
A Mitosis of the Spirit

> L'audace de la langue, le symbolisme, le glissement vers le fantastique, une tendresse tout à fait contraire aux tendances européenes actuelles apparentent *L'aventure ambiguë* au *Regard du roi* de Laye Camara.[10]
>
> The audacity of the language, the symbolism, the sliding toward the fantastic, a tenderness that is completely contrary to contemporary European tendencies link *Ambiguous Adventure* to Camara Laye's [Radiance of the King].

Cheikh Hamidou Kane's *Ambiguous Adventure* (1963) is linked to *The Radiance of the King* by many similarities in addition to those of style and tone. Both novels display strong Islamic influence. In both works the protagonist is driven to achieve unity with God. Camara Laye's protagonist, Clarence, seeks a personal coherence and spiritual union that he has never known. Samba Diallo of *Ambiguous Adventure* seeks to return to a former purity, a oneness with God and the universe that he has lost since leaving Africa. His ambiguous adventure is a calculated risk, learning the ways of the West in order to combat them for the sake of his people. Eventually he undergoes the deeply upsetting experience of a painful division of mind from spirit. He must struggle to regain the mystical unity he has known in his youth.

Cheikh Hamidou Kane, himself now a Senegalese government official, has experienced, as Camara Laye did, the three worlds of traditional Islamic Africa, Paris student life, and modern African government ministries. Like his hero, Samba Diallo, Kane studied first at a village Koranic school, then at a colonial French school in Senegal, then in Paris at the Sorbonne. He is now a specialist in economics.[11] As should become clear, Samba Diallo does not speak for Kane, but there are parallels that suggest that Kane writes of the been-to's crisis of conscience with some personal familiarity.

The European protagonist of *The Radiance of the King* achieves his spiritual union in ambiguous terms. The final embrace with the King moves beyond the novel's realism. We can interpret the act only symbolically. In *Ambiguous Adventure*, Samba Diallo's reunion with the absolute occurs only after his death. The final chapter, also disengaged from Western realism, allows a symbolic expression of Sufism finally to emerge as a dominant mode. *Ambiguous Adventure* "is basically the philosophic and religious expression of a people whose concepts and idiom are . . . alien to ours; and it would be impossible for them to phrase their thoughts in any way that was not strange to us," writes Katherine Woods, the translator of the novel from French to English.[12]

Of the many works that employ the been-to convention, *Ambiguous Adventure* is the most concise and provides one of the most intense statements of the issues. Although the novel deals with personal division and cultural fragmentation, the work itself is a self-contained and internally consistent whole despite its French, Islamic, and African influences. Kane directs the unifying elements of the novel—plot, setting, image, characterization, and symbol—toward the embodiment of the theme of Samba Diallo's internalized conflict between Africa and the West. The novel subordinates experience to theme. Dramatic illusions of experience are few. Incident plays a diminished role in the novel, serving primarily to set the stage for dialogue. And, in fact, the dialogue often gives way to a single character's extended disquisition on some aspect of African spirituality. The narrator asserts this point clearly:

The story of Samba Diallo is a serious story. If it had been a gay recital, we should have told you of the two white children, on the first morning of their sojourn among little Negroes, in finding themselves in the presence of so many black faces. . . .

But nothing more will be said of all that because these memories would revive others, also happy, and would bring a gaiety to this recital of which the truth is profoundly sad.[13]

Kane's intention to focus on the protagonist's tormenting dilemma becomes apparent soon enough. The need for the authorial interjection is doubtful. The style, moreover, is generally elliptic, eliminating almost all details that do not elucidate the central elements of the been-to's conflict. What Kane holds back—that which is not said—creates a quality of reserve which is wholly appropriate to the novel. Robert Pageard describes this trait eloquently:

L'aventure ambiguë est un livre de grande noblesse. Il en emane une tristesse qui est le fruit de siecles de meditation statique. Cette faible mobilité s'exprime dans le style, caracterisé par la retenue de l'expression, des chapelets de silences.[14]

Ambiguous Adventure is a work of great nobility. There emanates from it a sadness which is the result of centuries of static meditation. This feeble mobility expresses itself in the style, characterized by the reticence of expression, of a string of silences.

The argument, as Wilfred Cartey points out, is one of extremes, again in keeping with the literary convention of the been-to. "Argumentation is not in relatives, but in finalities."[15] And the contention is between opposing forces that can yield no quarter. The struggle that takes place within Samba Diallo's sensibilities is not a case in which the extent to which he becomes Westernized equals the extent to which he is de-Africanized. His dilemma has a dual complexity. He voices two complaints:

"I am not a distinct country of the Diallobé facing a distinct occident and appreciating that which I must take from it and what I must leave with it by way of counter balance. I have become the two. There is not a clear mind decided between the two factors of a choice. There is a strange nature and in distress over not being two." [P. 140]
"I no longer burn at the heart of men and things." [P. 150]

The anguish he feels in not being a clear mind deciding between two choices suggests what is in fact the case, that he is neither one nor the other; this condition generates his second complaint, the loss of his one-ness with the physical together with the spiritual worlds. The novel's focus never moves from this issue. The austere selection that shapes *Ambiguous Adventure* elicits the convention's most elegant expression of the been-to's African/Occident crisis. Or, as Cartey notes, "The action of the novel describes an arc which leads downward to silences and increasing bouts of trembling, to deepening anguish and an increasing sense of ambiguity."[16]

The plot is very simple. Because of his intellectual and spiritual promise, Samba Diallo, a young cousin of the leader of the Diallobé people, is sent from his home in Senegal to study in Paris. In this case, the Diallobé plan to combat the West by learning its techniques goes awry. The same intense intelligence that has made Samba Diallo an outstanding Koranic student makes him an equally adept disciple of Western abstract thought. Before his education is complete, his father recalls him to the country of the Diallobé, where he returns, now equally drawn to contradictory Western and African values. Shortly after his return he is killed by the Fool, a countryman who mistakes Samba Diallo's struggle of conscience for an act of impiety.

Nothing extraneous obtrudes. Although he is attracted to two young women, romance is only very slightly hinted at. He does not plan a revolution, nor is he tempted to amass any great wealth. Kane's protagonist is of a singular turn. In the country of the Diallobé, that trait manifests itself in a spiritual passion. In the West, it expresses itself in Samba Diallo's fascination with rationalism, spiritualism's polar opposite. Only in the realm beyond death "where there is no ambiguity" are the opposites reconciled.

Although the ambiguity of Samba Diallo's adventure derives in large measure from contrast of places, setting in the novel is treated in minimal detail. As he does with his plot, Kane restricts the details of setting so that his theme may remain paramount. Kane's land of the Diallobé is almost invisible to his readers. Such specific imagery as "swallows fluttering among the smoke-blackened lattices of the thatched roof" (p. 26) are few. In fact, Kane's most detailed African images are not those of the African landscape itself, but of sunset or nightfall above it.

On the horizon it seemed as if the earth were poised on the edge of an abyss. Above the abyss the sun was suspended, dangerously. The liquid silver of its heat had been reabsorbed. Only, the air was tinted with red, and under this illumination the little town seemed suddenly to belong to a strange planet. [P. 68]

Watching this sunset, the French schoolmaster is troubled, sensing limits to his reason to answer the mysteries of experience. Samba Diallo's father, the Knight, tells him, "When the sun dies, no scientific certainty should keep us from weeping for it. No rational evidence should keep us from asking that it be reborn. You are slowly dying under the weight of evidence. I wish you that anguish like a resurrection" (p. 71).

In an earlier scene, perhaps during the same sunset, Samba Diallo and Lacroix's son, Jean, are similarly moved. As twilight falls, Samba Diallo must pray.

His long white caftan—turned violet now by the evening light, was swept through by a kind of shiver which grew more pronounced in measure as [his] voice [in prayer] was rising. The shiver became a tremor which shook his entire body and the voice turned to a sob. To the east the sky was like an immense lilac-colored crystal. [P. 55]

Later, the French boy wonders fearfully why Samba Diallo had wept at the coming of night. In these two scenes, the landscape functions symbolically, for the characters as well as for the reader. Through the immense, yet ephemeral, twilight the Diallobés apprehend the presence of God. The French are also stirred but have no answers to the questions the evening arouses in them.

In those portions of the novel set in France, the landscape is presented in similarly subjective terms. Kane's images of Paris are mechanistic, reiterating the Fool's impressions of the West as a land of the triumphant, hard surface, sterile and menacing. "This valley of stone was traversed on its axis by a river of wild and head-strong mechanisms" (p. 84). In the oppressive heat of Paris in late June, Samba Diallo perceives the Boulevard Saint-Michel as populated with "objects of flesh . . . as well as objects of metal" (p. 119). He perceives the West as a place where events occur so rapidly as to congest time itself. "Time is obstructed by their mechanical jumble," he tells himself.

Kane uses setting to impart to Africa a deeply moving sense of mystery, the Divine Presence, and the vital human spirit. He depicts Paris, on the other hand, as a frightening mechanical creation that demonstrates the limits and dangers of pure reason.[17] After his return to Senegal, another sunset and twilight painfully remind Samba Diallo of his youthful spiritual purity as he discovers that he cannot bring himself to pray.

The setting of the final chapter is the world beyond death. In this waterlike realm, there is no light or darkness or weight or ambiguity. Here, Samba Diallo is reborn to being, free of the conflicts that have divided him, for there are no irreconcilables here. Kane employs this setting, a sea of infinity, equally to resolve his protagonist's dilemma and to assert its insolubility in human life.

As he does with the other unifying devices of the novel, Kane also puts characterization to the service of his theme. Rather than fully developed personalities, the characters of *Ambiguous Adventure* are embodiments of ideas. Each represents some philosophical position along a continuum of argument. The priestly Thierno represents one extreme, and the anonymous Parisians, whom Samba and the Fool perceive as machinelike objects, the other.

The frail, leaflike Thierno is emblematic of the Islamic spiritual ideal. Although he realistically recognizes that other people must make practical concessions, he allows himself none. The revered Koranic teacher aspires to the weightlessness of pure spirit.

> Weight! Everywhere he encountered weight. When he wanted to pray, weight opposed him, the heavy load of his daily cares over the upward sweep of his thought toward God, the inert and more and more sclerotic mass of his body over his will to rise, then to abase himself then to rise again in the notions of prayer. [Pp. 29–30]

The priestlike teacher is given to rage if a pupil forgets a lesson. Because he sees Samba as especially gifted, he treats him with special cruelty for minor lapses. He pinches through the flesh of Samba's ear lobe and scorches the boy's flesh with burning faggots. "But while his hand was threatening, his eager gaze was full of admiration and his attention drank in the words the little boy spoke. What purity! What a miracle!" (p. 5). And he is equally without concern for the comfort of his own body.

> The crackling of all his joints, stiff rheumatism, made a sound which was mingled with the sigh wrested from him by the effort to get up. . . . The teacher was rising to pray—the teacher could not restrain an inner laughter over this grotesque misery of his body. . . . "You will get up and you will pray," he said to himself. "Your groanings and your noises will avail you nothing." [P. 26]

The greatest teacher of the Koran in the country of the Diallobé, he is sought after for edification by other teachers, even from great distances. All the distinguished families seek the honor of enrolling their children as students in his school of the Glowing Hearth. But, he says, "I am nothing, . . . only a minute echo which claimed while it lasted to be swollen with the Word . . . the Word weaves together what is, more intimately than the light weaves the day" (p. 110).

Despite his commitment to his mystic meditations upon the beauties of the Koran, Thierno knows privately of the Diallobés' need to live in this world; he understands that his quest for personal purity is a dangerous model for the Diallobé.

> "Your house is the most scantily furnished in the countryside, your body the most emaciated, your appearance the most fragile. But no one has a sovereign authority over this country which equals yours," [the Most Royal Lady tells him.]
>
> The teacher felt terror overcoming him. . . . He had never dared to admit very plainly what she was saying, but he knew it to be the truth. [P. 32]

Thierno sees the threat of the West, which would end the material poverty of his people but, at the same time, would destroy their spirituality. So he consents to give up Samba Diallo, his most extraordinarily gifted pupil in forty years' teaching so that, armed with a Western education, Samba might become the Diallobés' weapon against the West. It is the Fool, an earlier traveler to the West, who assesses the circumstances and the teacher's role accurately. "It is only your survival that delays the metamorphosis," he tells the Koranic Master (p. 80).

As the survivor of an earlier epoch, the teacher feebly resists the tide of the occidental culture. Between him and the new world are the Knight, Samba Diallo's father, and Samba's cousin, the Most Royal Lady. The Knight, "the articulator of the dilemma of the Western World, of its problems"[18] is a devout Moslem. Cartey notes that the Knight's physical proportions are reflective of his mental state. The Knight is tall, large, and of noble bearing. To the Frenchman, Lacroix, he resembles a medieval knight. The Knight, a proponent of syncretism, believes that people cannot live with separate destinies and "sees history as providence and as a movement toward a fated end."[19] As a Moslem, the Knight lives for the end of the world, the idea of which Kane presents through the spectacular sunset. He debates with Lacroix, the Westerner whose rational processes fail to pierce the meaning of the coming of the night, or more specifically the end of the world. Lacroix argues, "The Universe which science has revealed to the West is less immediately human, but confess that it is more solid." And the Knight counters, "It has reconquered that world from chaos. But, I believe that in so doing it has laid you open to despair" (p. 70).

On the other hand, the world of Islam "believes in the end of the world . . . at the same time that it hopes for it and fears it." He deplores the Western separation of fact from spirit. He tells Lacroix:

"From the bottom of my heart I wish for you to discover the feeling of anguish in the face of the dying sun. I ardently wish that for the West. When the sun dies, no scientific certainty should keep us from weeping for it, no rational evidence should keep us from asking that it might be reborn. You are slowly dying under the weight of evidence. I wish you that anguish—like a resurrection."

"To what shall we be reborn?" [the Westerner asks.]

"To a more profound truth. Evidence is a quality of the surface. Your science is the triumph of evidence, a proliferation of the surface. It makes you masters of the external, but at the same time, it exiles you there, more and more." [P. 71]

"My father does not live, he prays," Samba says of him (p. 87) and then is shocked by his own idea in which life and prayer are opposed. The passing idea foreshadows the dualism that is later to develop in Samba. For the Knight, while fine distinctions can be made between matters of spirit and mind, the presence of God pervades all spheres. "There are those who believe and those who do not believe, the division is clear. It leaves no one outside its neatly drawn line" (p. 93). The Knight's serenity, deriving from his emotional containment in the world of the Diallobé, offers the growing Samba Diallo the surety that his Koranic teacher's words once afforded. Samba has yet to learn of the limits of his father's vision. In the end, the Knight sees his error. He writes to recall his son from France.

It is high time that you should come back, to learn that God is not commensurable with anything, and especially not with history, whose vicissitudes are powerless in relations to His attributes. I know that the Occident, to which I have been so wrong as to send you, has a different faith on that score but . . . Between God and man there exists not the slightest consanguinity, nor do I know what historic relationship. [P. 151].

The Western Scar

The Most Royal Lady represents a somewhat more worldly spirituality, one of physical life that seeks to accommodate the exigencies. Sister to the chief, able to control the rebellious outlying tribes by the force of her majesty, she is determined not to lose to the colonialists. How was it that her grandfather, whose arm was strengthened by his total belief in the righteousness of his cause, was conquered by the invading Europeans? She is eager to learn their secret "art of conquering without being in the right" (p. 33). She sees a key to power in abstraction and technological skill. She understands that the Diallobés' spiritualism cannot withstand the spiritless material might of the West. The Most Royal Lady recognizes that she recommends a dangerous course. But she is convinced that the only way to stop the Western conquest, continuing now not on the land but within the minds and spirits of the Diallobés, will be to learn Western ways. She tells her people, "I, the Most Royal Lady, do not like the foreign school. . . . My opinion, nevertheless, is that we should send our children there" (p. 14).

She likens the children of the Diallobé to their best fields ploughed up and burned off and to their best seeds, planted away for future harvest. "The school in which I would place our children will kill in them what today we love and rightly conserve with care. Perhaps the very memory of us will die in them" (p. 42).

Given the dangers facing the Diallobés, the Most Royal Lady acts without faith. She cannot be certain that her choice will not be the ruin of her people. Yet the dangers of metamorphosis represented by the new school are not fully clear to her. It seems to her that even though the new crop that the school will produce may be somewhat different from the rest of the tribespeople, the children will still be Diallobés. Like her brother, she does not fully see the metaphysical dangers in her proposal. In order that the people will participate in the calculated risk, she persuades the Chief that their young cousin, Samba Diallo, should be the first to enroll in the foreign school.

The Most Royal Lady, the Knight, and the teacher embody differing degrees of Islamic Africanity. The West has touched them only lightly. However, they are aware that it represents a powerful danger. Other characters in the novel, Westerners or Africans who live in the West or who have returned, similarly embody philosophical positions. Some unequivocally embody the support of Western materialism. Others knowingly or unknowingly represent the dangers of concession.

Pierre Lacroix, the French master of the foreign school, argues for the solidity of science. His faith rests in the material products of science. His unquestioned conviction of the world's reality is quite unlike the equally unquestioned African perception of what is real. Lacroix studies the Knight, who is moved to evening prayer at the setting sun.

> Behind it an imposing mass of bright red cloud had come crumbling down like a monstrous stream of clotted blood. The red splendor of the air had been progressively softened under the impact of the slow invasion of the evening shade.
>
> Strange, Lacroix was thinking, this fascination of nothingness for those who have nothing. . . . They call it the absolute. They turn their backs to the light but they look at the shadow fixedly. Is it that this man is not conscious of his poverty? [P. 72]

Pierre-Louis is an aging black man whom Samba Diallo meets in Paris. He has served as magistrate in French courts and as advocate for his compatriots in colonial states. "I know now the reason for this old man's madness," Samba Diallo said to himself. "He has been too clear-headed through the course of a too long life" (p. 140). Pierre-Louis dreams of liberty and imagines himself a revolutionary even though, as a member of the bar, he has had to make his peace with France. He describes himself as "a lion that you have before you, monsieur, a lion that roars and leaps forward everytime a blow is struck in the sacred cause of liberty" (p. 124). But Samba Diallo, who can imagine what concessions the "lion" has made, sees him as the "passion of the revolution as well as its mad dreams" (ibid.). The West has its many techniques for dealing with its enemies. Pierre-Louis's necessary accommodations of his revolutionary fervor illustrate the Diallobés' dilemma. Although the Knight may carefully speak of parallels in Christianity with his own religious philosophies, even while he cautions Samba of the dangers of his foreign venture, he believes that a process of syncretism is possible. He hopes that the cultural interchange will bring about a renaissance of spirituality in the West. But he speaks from within the relative security of his Islamic convictions and the comforting surrounding world of Senegal. On the other hand, Pierre-Louis has been engaged in active psychological combat and has lost. Through his example, Samba Diallo comes to understand the folly of the Diallobés' plan. Pierre-Louis, who has become a black Frenchman and whose resistance has become a meaningless posture, demonstrates the apparent invulnerability of the West.

The Western Scar

Lucienne Martial, a young Frenchwoman in Samba's classes in philosophy at the Sorbonne, represents a philosophical position somewhat similar to that of Pierre-Louis. She argues that "the possession of God ought not cost man any of his chances" (p. 108). But she is the daughter of a Protestant minister and at the same time a member of the Communist Party. Samba admires her "spiritual adventure," that is, the arduous process of reconciling her Christian faith with Marxist materialism. However, "it did not seem to [him] that he would have had the sweep of mind to go through such an adventure." For Samba, religious commitment should be a matter of choice. To choose one thing is also to reject other things.

It would have been better, he thinks, had the African been given the opportunity for such a choice and have chosen religious faith over material development and physical health. Instead, any spiritual benefits deriving from European presence in Africa are tempered by the new emphases on materialism that the Westerners have brought with them.

Part of Samba's trial in the West is to resist the path of accommodation offered to him in the examples of people he meets. Many of Kane's Westerners operate by choosing not to look too closely at inherent contradictions in their convictions about moral and material issues. However, the Fool, a Diallobé who has returned from the West, lacks the psychological agility to sustain conflicting values. His stay in the West has been a terrifying experience. After an absence of several years, he has returned, bearing a scar on his abdomen and a compulsion to tell how he was wounded. Finally, during one of his neurotic recitals, he collapses and utters what sounds like a death rattle. Thereafter, he is avoided by his tribespeople, but he is compelled to seek them out to tell his story. Like the ancient mariner, the Fool is a classic been-to. Bearing his Western scar, he is trapped in the harsh memories of his metamorphosing experience. He sees the Western world as an "obscene chaos" filled with deadly spaces. "Mechanisms are reigning there" (p. 84).

Since the Fool is mad, we assume he does not represent Kane's particular view of the West. Yet, the author presents the Fool's views as one kind of response the West can evoke. The Fool's vision is the most extremely negative reaction to the Occident in the novel and, indeed, is one of the strongest attacks on the West in the entire literary convention of the been-to. He envisions a world of unyielding hard surfaces where humans have been transformed into monstrosities encased in hard shells:

On the hard asphalt, my exacerbated ears and my eager eyes were vainly on the lookout for the soft upheaval of earth from a naked foot. There was no foot anywhere around me. On the hard carapace there was only the clattering of a thousand hard shells. Had men no longer feet of flesh? A woman passed me, the pink flesh of her calves hardened monstrously in two black terminal conches at the level of the asphalt. . . .

"Master" [he tells the teacher], "I would like to pray with you . . . to repeal the upheaval. There is obscene chaos in the world once more and it defies us." [P. 83]

Although Samba Diallo eventually, albeit briefly, concurs in the Fool's perception of Europe, he can never reject it in the whole-hearted manner of his countryman. For he has been fatally taken by a "foreign philosophy . . . seductive lines of thought and chains of pure logic . . . abstract ideas [and] disembodied concepts."[20] At the early stages of his European education, he voices his fears of the danger of metamorphosis he faces. "We are turned into hybrids and there we are left," he says, "then we hide ourselves filled with shame." But the very intensity that has so impressed the Koranic Master is his undoing. He enters the West ill-equipped for his venture. He learns too late that he should have developed much greater reserve. Having loved the Koranic Word "for its mystery and somber beauty," having absorbed the Divine Presence from the world around him, he remains too receptive to Europe's intellectual appeals.

Before he is to leave for Europe, he passes the ritual Night of the Koran, during which he recites for his parents the entire holy book from memory. Although generations of his ancestors have performed the ceremony, he understands that he is bringing the tradition to its close.

But he considered that it was important for him, more than for any of those who preceded him to acquit himself to the full on his Night. For it seemed to him that this Night marked an end. The scintillation of the heavens above his head, was it not the star-studded bolt being drawn upon an epoch that had run its course? [P. 66]

History determines that Samba Diallo must leave the past that would have led to a life as a Sufi Master. Instead, he takes on a far more significant role, participant in a mythic quest. Even though his venture leaves him at the end of his life in an unfinished hybrid state, he achieves an epic significance. As one critic puts it, "The hero's experience consists in the inner dialogue of his conscience with itself yet it retains a universal quality, the myth transposed to intellectual level, of the 'quest for the . . . Holy Grail.' "[21]

Samba Diallo continues to offer prayers that set him apart from others while he is in Europe. Even though he continues to "live his death" focused in spirit on Allah, there is too much to resist. Even though he "resists the temptation to follow the beautiful but false gods of liberty, revolution, culture, even though he resists the appeals of négritude,"[22] he suffers from the absence of the context of the Word of the Koran. "The Word weaves together what is, more intimately than the light weaves the day. The Word overflows your destiny," Kane tells us (p. 110).

Out of the stable, structured tribal society, he suffers in the pragmatic world without context that he perceives the West to be.[23] Rowing in midstream, he stops his boat to say, "I should have wished that the heat of the sun would suddenly abate, the sky would become more blue and the water of the river would flow more swiftly and make more sound. The universe ought to scintillate all around us" (p. 134). He understands the process at work in him. Having stepped out of a structure of belief, he has lost "a privileged mode of acquaintance" with reality (p. 139). His psychological travels are among the furthest of any been-to of the literary convention.

He continues to recognize that to choose Allah is to reject the world. However, the world obtrudes, seemingly even while he continues to choose Allah. Even though the paradox is different from not having chosen Allah, the results for Samba Diallo are nonetheless specific.

> He enters into the dark night of a metaphysical solitude from which he will later try, by various routes, to escape. . . . The real exile [he] undergoes in Europe is his failure any longer to feel the Divine Presence. True, the God of Pascal is also perceptible to the heart, but strict Christian orthodoxy—if orthodoxy has any place in mysticism—allows of no psychological reaction either guaranteeing or measuring the presence of God. But, with all the importance he attaches to feeling, it is nevertheless Samba Diallo for whom the Absolute is wholly and eternally transcendant.[24]

Recalled to the Diallobé by his father, he returns, bearing like the Fool a Western scar from his psychological wound. Cut off from the West, unable to be at one with his people, he takes an iron comfort in the Fool's ritual execration against the West.

"Master, they have no more bodies, they have no more flesh. They have been eaten up by objects. In order that they may move, their bodies are shod with large rapid objects. To nourish themselves, they put iron objects between their hands and mouths. . . ."

"That is indeed true," said Samba Diallo, thoughtfully. [P. 158]

Although the Fool sees Samba Diallo confusedly as the new Koranic Master, or as the old master returned from the dead, Samba Diallo cannot lead him in prayer as the Fool implores him to do. "Let us pray. Oh, let us pray. . . . If we do not pray, the hour [of twilight] will pass" (p. 161).

As the Fool leads him to the grave mounds of the city of the dead, Samba struggles to regain his Islamic faith through his reasoning powers. He addresses the dead master in his thoughts: "I do not believe very much any more, of what you have taught me. I do not know what I believe. But the extent is so vast, of what I do not know, and what I ought indeed to believe" (p. 161).

Samba Diallo's intensive study of Pascal, Descartes, Socrates, and St. Augustine have borne a result, a mind divorced from spirit. Whereas as a child he wept his prayers on these same graves in a total unity of feeling and belief, he now attempts to pick his return to spiritual belief through the careful steps of private rational discourse.

Athough it is dubious that Samba Diallo's reason can lead him back to his earlier unquestioning faith, he maintains the hope that it will. As Clarence of *The Radiance of the King* does in his moments of spiritual crisis, Samba Diallo takes comfort in the thought that his good will must be credited. He believes he has seen the way out of his crisis: "To constrain God . . . to give Him the choice between His return within your heart and your death, in the name of His glory . . . he cannot evade the choice, if I constrain Him, truly, from the bottom of my heart, with all I have of sincerity" (p. 162).

The Fool continues to urge him to pray, shocked at Samba Diallo's seeming impiety during the hour of prayer. Samba Diallo silently reasons, "I will not agree . . . to suffer from thy withdrawal." Not hearing the Fool's frenzied urgings to prayer and not realizing that he speaks aloud, Samba says, "No—I do not agree." The Fool, thinking that Samba rebukes him, draws a weapon (a sword, a club, a gun brought back from the West?) and kills Samba.

The final chapter of the novel is one of reconciliation as Samba travels in the furthest reaches of the been-to's mythic journey, now not an underworld of Western demons or malevolent spirits or obscene mechanisms. The scene is the waterworld of Islamic spirituality wherein all ambiguity ends in a realm beyond divisions. " 'Be attentive', a voice says, 'for see, you are reborn to being. There is no more light, there is no more weight, the darkness is no more. Feel how antagonisms do not exist' " (p. 164). Like Clarence, he merges with the infinite, past all limitations of his mind and senses.

The nature of Samba Diallo's death, and therefore something of the novel's meaning, has been a source of confusion. One critic sees the death as metaphoric, perhaps, not real. Perhaps Samba Diallo merely loses consciousness. His unconscious spirituality, long held in check by a powerful rational mind overly developed in the West, is once again freed to assert its ascendancy.[25] But the nature of the final chapter leaves no doubt that Samba Diallo is dead. And, as we shall see, Kane himself corroborates this contention.

Jeanne-Lydic Gore concludes that Samba Diallo chose to have himself put to death by the Fool, that he deliberately goads the madman to release him from the pains of his ambiguous state. As justification for his conclusion that Samba Diallo's death is self-willed, Gerald Moore cites Mme. Gore's quotation from Chibli, "Celui qui est habitué à Ton intimité, ne supporte l'éloignement. Celui que a été touché au coeur par Ton amour, ne peut supporter meme la proximité. Si l'oeil ne Te voit pas, le coeur T'a déjà vu."[26] "He who is accustomed to intimacy with Thee cannot stand separation. He whose heart has been touched by Thy love could not stand even mere proximity. If the eye does not see Thee, the heart already has." Moore writes, "In this light, his suicide itself becomes explicable, almost acceptable."[27]

In response to Jeanne-Lydic Gore, Cheikh Hamidou Kane himself has said, "I don't know, I'm not sure myself, I cannot say definitely whether Samba Diallo committed suicide, whether he deliberately arranged to be killed."[28] The disclaimer is hard to accept. The novel is a far too structured sequence of logically related ideas to suggest that Kane writes as a sensitive lyre blown by mysterious winds. But intention or the author's decision in retrospect notwithstanding, the context of the novel is clear. Samba Diallo speaks from the conviction that his withdrawal from God is impermanent. His "No, I do not agree" is only an assertion of the intensity of that conviction, not an attempt to goad the Fool to act. Moreover, it would be entirely out of character for him to exploit the Fool by deliberately inflicting such pain upon him as to drive him to murder. His death has another meaning, philosophical, not psychological.

In this respect, the reticence of the novel is significant. Intent upon his theme, Kane withholds a good deal of Samba Diallo's experiences. Such events are not part of *Ambiguous Adventure* simply because of the novel's philosophical intent. For example, Kane's characters seem to encounter one another primarily to hone their ideas. Social intercourse is secondary. Robert Pageard's reference to "chapelets de silences," quoted earlier in this section, is helpful to our understanding of the novel.

The silences that the work seems to create derive from Kane's elliptical technique. He omits details that would shift attention from the religious and philosophical theme. The reader is privy to very few of Samba Diallo's feelings concerning matters of daily life. Lucienne's appealing glances and shy touches may indeed have their effect, for she and Samba remain friends. But we never learn. We do learn that Adele's beauty awakens emotions he immediately regrets. Samba primly reprimands himself, calling himself "Mbara," a slave name his parents applied to him when they wished to shame him for bad behavior. Although he and Adele walk the quays of Paris arm in arm, we learn no more of his feelings for her. Instead, that scene focuses on Samba's thoughts of the growing distance between himself and God. Neither do we know of his feelings for home and his family. In short, Kane admits his readers only to those carefully constructed details that set forth his version of the been-to's crisis of conscience.

Given, then, that *Ambiguous Adventure* is a philosophical novel with a limited intent, it is apparent that the protagonist's death serves as more than a logical end of a sequence of events generated by character and circumstance. *Ambiguous Adventure* sets in opposition two philosophical concepts and embodies them both in Samba Diallo. His person, or perhaps more precisely, his conflict could serve as a synecdoche. He embodies the conflicting propositions—(1) that the mind is the route to salvation and (2) that the intuitive spirit is the route to salvation. Simultaneously he represents the most refined European sensibility and the most intense African sensibility. Like other been-to novels, *Ambiguous Adventure* presents the mythic battle within the spirit of one who partakes of two worlds with equal intensity.

Although Africa and the West are presented in very broad terms, the West is not seen as merely aspiring toward a transcendant mechanization, nor is Africa seen as most truly represented by spiritual aspirations. On the contrary, Western spiritualism is represented by Paul Martial, the Protestant pastor who reminds Samba Diallo of the teacher of the Diallobé. And the Diallobé leaders know that the power that the Occident holds over Africa is as a source of material goods. Nonetheless, Kane has formulated a dramatic abstraction of the fundamental aspects of the genuine disjunction between Africa and the Occident.

Samba Diallo's death seems to assert that there is no reconciliation for his conflict in this life. The reconciliation occurs beyond the human sphere. Samba's death does not alter the human problem. Yet Cheikh Hamidou Kane says:

> I am not sure that we Africans have succeeded yet in achieving the synthesis either in our national life or in our daily lives as individuals. I think, though, that it is something that we have to achieve. . . . [I]f I had any object in writing my novel it was to try to find out whether such a synthesis was conceivable.[29]

James Olney points out that *Ambiguous Adventure* demonstrates that conflicts irreconcilable in life can have their solutions in the realm of art. Yet *Ambiguous Adventure* is not irrelevant to life. Samba Diallo's "cartesian dualism" is one stage of growth.[30] The Most Royal Lady's image of the young generation as seeds for a future harvest of metamorphosed Africans is accurate.

Fragments:
Disorder Transcendant

Even though Kane's lyric novel symbolizes Africa's vast historic transition, its attention remains focused upon the crisis of religious sensibility. In contrast, Ayi Kwei Armah's *Fragments*, while it achieves a similar emotional intensity, nevertheless presents a broader, more realistic point of view of contemporary West Africa. Moreover, although the graphic social realism of *Fragments* bitterly satirizes the serious shortcomings of the struggling new nation of Ghana, Armah artfully exploits the poetic potentials of his story to extend the meanings of the been-to convention and to intensify its impact. In fact, *Fragments* represents the most fully developed, artful usage of the been-to convention in all West African fiction.

Baako Onipe's return from the West remains the central issue throughout the novel. In the first two chapters the return is anticipated. The third chapter tells of his flight from Paris to Accra and his arrival at home. All that follows stems from this event. Baako's impressions of the Ghana that has developed during his absence, his relatives' reactions to him, and the effects that his experiences as a been-to have upon him are the substance of *Fragments*. The hostility that Baako develops against Ghanaian society produces an intensely experienced struggle. His attempts to retain his identity finally promise an eventual victory over despair and madness. The journey in *Fragments* is more metaphorical than actual. Baako's Western journey ends as the novel begins; his psychological journey, however, is just getting under way. He must continue to explore the new state of being that his Western education has imperfectly presented to him. No longer a traditional African, yet rejecting Western values, he is in a state of anomy. He perceives the world outside himself as fragmented. His emotional collapse, which affirms and intensifies his alienation, forces his continued quest. To survive, Baako must restructure the world within his own consciousness, using where he can the fragments of the world he has known. To determine what has happened to himself, he must determine what has happened to his society. This second journey, the psychological mythic quest, does not end with the novel. Baako does not actually become the transcendant been-to. He does, however, achieve a powerful unifying understanding that is forced into existence by the intensity of his experience. The novel ends with hope for his success.

In the end, he has traveled farther than Obi Okonkwo or Samba Diallo. Their symbolic travels stop far short of the point that Baako reaches. Obi does not marry Clara; Samba returns to the Diallobé. Neither Achebe nor Kane has his hero venture beyond a critical limit defined for him by his family. In Achebe's case, the decision reflects, in part, the limits of the author's own vision of the meaning of the been-to. Although the cautionary tale of the wrestler who ventured into the spirit world is suggested more than once, Achebe has acknowledged that he did not consciously consider the parallels to Obi's story. Obi's adventure in the spirit world occurred in the author's unconscious and is only suggested in *No Longer at Ease*. In *Ambiguous Adventure*, the issue concerns Samba Diallo's spirituality. The metaphysical element is expressed in his metamorphosis into two things. When he understands how he has "become two," Samba tries to return to his former state.

Armah, on the other hand, carries the venture further. In his madness, Baako thinks of himself as one who has gone into the world of spirits and has returned as a kind of ghost, even as a kind of god.[31] Through this device, Armah consciously develops his protagonist's significance to something greater than the typical young Ghanaian of the seventies or even the typical African of this century. Baako approaches the status of the mythic hero who struggles to create a new identity in the chaos of rapidly continuing events.

Fragments is Armah's second novel. Like his first, *The Beautyful Ones Are Not Yet Born*, it is deeply concerned with the social issues of Ghana of the 1960s. Because the moral and political tone of the second novel is a development of matters introduced in his first, we shall consider briefly some of the concerns of *The Beautyful Ones Are Not Yet Born*.

The unnamed hero of Armah's first novel ("the man"), while not a been-to, is like many been-tos in the West African convention, an indigenous stranger, alienated by the corruption in his society. Adhering to a private moral aesthetic, he is forced into greater and greater isolation despite his understanding of the need for social communion.[32] *The Beautyful Ones Are Not Yet Born* has been described as "not so much about a person as it is . . . about a society with the protagonist definitely *outside* the situation, that is the hero as voyeur."[33] Forced into his position by his moral values, the man is indeed an onlooker. But he cannot ever completely withdraw from society, for he has a wife and children. His responsibility for them forces him to participate in a culture he deplores. There is no escape, for he is an ordinary railway clerk with no special skills or extraordinary courage that would permit him to start life somewhere else. Moreover, he has the disquieting example of his mentor, the Teacher, who has withdrawn from the world, but recognizies that his position renders him impotent to effect any change in the society he condemns. The novel is then in fact very much about a man. Its action is internal and intense and concerns society only in that it deals with the issue of living in that society.[34] Although *The Beautyful Ones Are Not Yet Born* is "rather humorless,"[35] it is not an expression of "hopeless despair," as it has been described.[36] The novel's imagery, expressive of Armah's "almost Swiftian preoccupation with the bodily secretions,"[37] suggests the author's intense feelings of revulsion in regard to Ghana, or more accurately, his protagonist's. Yet, Camara Laye's assertion that the African literary tradition is always optimistic seems to be borne out. As depressing as Armah finds West Africa, his first novel ends with the hope that the "beautyful ones" are yet to be born. The transitional period, during which the colonial exploiters have been replaced by equally exploitative Africans, will eventually end. Living perpetually at odds with his society may be "the man's" fate but perhaps not the fate of Ghanaians to come.

A similar kind of qualified optimism emerges in the final pages of *Fragments*. Armah again suggests that his hero lives during a difficult period of cultural transition which is eventually to end. In the meantime, however, the social problems of the region are deep-seated and major.

From the points of view of varied characters, Armah develops a composite of images of Ghanaian life which conveys a complex truth.[38] Baako, whose name vaguely reiterates throughout the novel his status as the newly returned, is the primary agency through which the theme of the cultural disorder of Ghana is presented. But the novel's minor characters serve this end as well. The first chapter consists of the unhappy ruminations of Baako's blind grandmother, Naana, who fears the demands his family will place upon him when he returns. Armah widens his scope in the second chapter. Through the perspective of Juana, a young Puerto Rican psychiatrist, he presents the chaotic, avaricious society of Accra, in which Baako is to make his way.

The third chapter, told from Baako's point of view, presents his homeward flight and his arrival in Accra. On the plane that brings him from Paris, he is accompanied by Brempong, the archetypal insensitive, materialistic been-to who has spent his time abroad getting rich and laying up a mass of impressive goods. He is the foil to Baako, who brings with him only his typewriter, a guitar, and an education that his countrymen will find of dubious value. Although the point of view shifts back to those of Juana and Naana later on, the greater part of the remainder of *Fragments* is told from Baako's point of view. As his family and his countrymen lead him more and more to see himself as a stranger in his own country, the reader is taken deeper and deeper in Baako's isolation.

Baako's emotional disorder is in large measure a reaction to a more widespread social disorder that Armah demonstrates in many aspects of Ghanaian life. A central core of spiritual or ethical value has almost died. Families, communities, religion, art, and politics are all affected by a pervasive obsession with commodity, which, as we shall see, Armah demonstrates is fast becoming the culture's highest value and prime mover.

Let us consider, then, how Armah treats the issue of disorder in varied aspects of Ghanaian national life. Naana, the blind grandmother, whose thoughts open the novel, represents, like Thierno of *Ambiguous*

Adventure, the failing strength of the Africa of rituals and belief. Her first thoughts, concerned with her absent grandson, begin the novel with the theme of the return.

> Each thing that goes away returns and nothing in the end is lost. The great friend throws all things apart and brings all things together again. That is the way everything goes and turns round. That is how all living things come back after long absences, and in the whole great world all things are living things. All that goes returns. He will return. [P. 11]

But the comfort that is afforded her by the traditional system of belief is undermined by her infirmities, which seem to call her convictions into question.[39] Her senses are failing her. She can no longer tell if she sits in sunlight or dark. Dependent on the love and care of others for her survival, she sees herself, and hence the values of her traditional world, as useless. Although she sees danger in the unwise new ways of her family, she does not speak of it.

> If I see things unseen by those who have eyes, why should my wisest speech be silence? . . . Their wishes are the closest thing they have to the beauty of long peaceful dreams, and in their wishing they too want this return. The things they want it for, the wishes below, those are the other things to load my soul with fear. [P. 13]

Thus, with his opening paragraphs, Armah introduces the central theme of the been-to's return to a difficult, materialistic culture. Even though Naana is disturbed that Baako's mother and sister are primarily interested in the wealth that they imagine his return will mean for them all, she is not above material ambitions for herself. If Baako has made his fortune, she counts on him not to forget her. Thus, although he is careful not to present Naana as a symbol of the old Africa of a lost idyllic world, Armah intends to show that in the new culture the order of the family structure is seriously threatened by the new appetite for goods.

Following Naana's uneasy summation of the state of affairs in Baako's family, Armah presents a signal image of equally disquieting conditions in the society at large. In *The Beautyful Ones Are Not Yet Born* Armah suggests that almost all Ghanaians are corrupt in one way or another. The protagonist and his mentor must seriously question whether sustaining their moral values does not represent selfish and even dangerous self-indulgence that radically separates them from their countrymen. In *Fragments* Armah demonstrates a greater sympathy for the common people, suggesting that their conditions are caused by external forces that mitigate against their normal fellow feeling.

Juana is a young psychiatrist who has come to Ghana eager to offer her professional services. But now, as the story develops, the unrelenting difficulties of West African life have grown wearing. She is plagued by recurrent desires for flight. Seeking the relief of country air, she drives out of Accra. On the outskirts of the city, she encounters more of the kind of experiences that make her stay in Ghana so taxing. Trying to avoid open gutters and the smell of sewage, she comes upon a group of men surrounding a shivering dog suspected of having rabies. A passionate cruelty sweeps through the group. The dog is beaten to death despite the pleas of the child who owns it. The brutal killing is a pleasure to the men, a release for private sufferings. Armah makes use of the cruelty of the scene, for it foreshadows Baako's treatment by his friends and family during his second mental collapse.[40] A sense of community is essential to the event. The men who kill the rabid dog risk a painful death, but the dog must be destroyed for the safety of others. Yet this scene does not evoke a positive sense of the community united to protect its members. The primary reactions Armah seeks to elicit are revulsion and apprehension. His "Swiftian preoccupation" with the liquids of the body is again evident. The dog's head is battered into an ooze of jellied brains and blood. When one of the killers triumphantly raises the dead dog's body aloft, he reveals himself as victim of some kind of suppurating genital malady. The bloodied dog's body drips as the man holds it up. "But from the man himself something else had commenced to drip: down along his right leg flowed a steam of something yellow like long-thickened urine mixed with streaks of clotted blood" (p. 38). In the old Africa, the sense of community is primary; ceremonies and rituals are enacted to promote order, procreation, and a sense of well-being.[41] In this passage, however, the powers of disorder are visibly at work. The participants are driven by private needs. The dog's madness is an occasion to release pent-up angers. The antithesis of a fertility ritual, the act of disorder ends with a killing and an ejaculation of poisonous humors.

Similarly, the force of disorder has also affected spiritual life. As she continues her drive, Juana encounters a "prophet" and his fanatical women followers, whom he baptizes naked in the sea. One of his followers is Efua, Baako's mother. She has come to the prophet to be led in prayers for the return of her son. Even though she believes in God, her prayers are merely self-serving. She is an example of the declining power of traditional religions, once a major source of African social coherence. "[He] went away to study. He will come back a man. A big man," she tells Juana proudly (p. 58). Later, when Baako has returned and Efua has no further need of the prophet, she no longer attends his ceremonies.[42]

Thus, when Baako appears in person in the third chapter of the narrative, the way has been prepared for him, and the reader has a sense of what awaits the been-to. On the plane, the politician, Brempong, tells him that when he saw Baako waiting in line to board, he was not certain that Baako was a fellow Ghanaian.

> "You look different somehow."
> "I never thought I looked so different."
> "I don't mean facially. But you know, how you're dressed, how you walk—you don't give the impression that you know you're a been-to. When a Ghanaian has had a chance to go abroad and is returning home its clear from any distance that he's a been-to coming back." [P. 76]

When Baako explains that he is nervous because, after five years abroad, he doesn't know what he will find at home, Brempong responds with pride.

> "Do you know how many years, total, I have spent out of Ghana?" Taking a deep puff on his cigarette, he leaned slowly back till his head touched the back of his seat and then he blew the smoke in a thin line directly into the light socket above him. "Do you know? Eight years total. Eight full years." [P. 73]

This contrast between the two men is significant. Brempong has the kind of high visibility that he thinks all been-tos should have. He lives on the surface and has a good time of it.

> "There are important things you can't get to buy at home," [he says.] "Everytime I go out I arrange to buy all I need, suits and so on. It's quite simple. I got two good cars on this trip. German cars, right from the factory all fresh. They're following me. Shipped. . . . You just have to know what to look for when you get a chance to go abroad. Otherwise, you come back empty handed like a fool, and all the time you spent is a waste, useless." [Pp. 73–74]

Baako's fears are not calmed by Brempong's comments, for he has little to bring back, not even any real prospects of work. At the airport no one greets him, for he has told no one of his coming. Brempong, on the other hand, is greeted by enthusiastic, praising relatives.

> "Eeeeei! Our white man, we saw you wave! We saw you!"
> "The big man has come again."
> "Oh, they have made you a white man."
> "Complete!"
> "And you have come back to us, your own. Thank God."
> "Yes, praise him!" [P. 88]

Brempong's sister regards Baako with suspicion. She cannot believe he is really a been-to, in his unprepossessing clothes, with his quiet diffidence.

This satirical passage dramatizes Baako's isolation, for Brempong's welcomers verify his opinion that one must play the role of the "big man" if he hopes to succeed in Ghana. Very likely the enthusiastic family would not be at the airport if Brempong were to arrive empty-handed. But, unlike Baako, Brempong moves and breathes with his society. Although his followers speak of his transformation, they are very like him, having developed similarly. He is eminently admired, for he can acquire the things they passionately long for. It is Baako who has been truly transformed. He ponders the difference between Brempong and himself.

> What power would Brempong find to sustain such a dizzy game? Or perhaps he had found as much of this power as was necessary. After all, the crowd [of greeters] around him had been just as willing to raise him skyward as he had been willing to let himself be lifted. Perhaps he was not likely to be worried about the power needed for this game, because like all the eager ones around him had had found in the game itself an easy potency he had not had to struggle for, to create. In spite of himself, Baako found a kind of fearful wonder invading him. A man had gone away, spent time elsewhere, grown months and years, and then returned. These he had left behind had spent time too, grown along their different waves, waiting to welcome thir traveller. In the end they had come waiting for him with a ceremony in their hearts, and amazingly it had happened that whatever strange ceremony he had been rehearsing inside his own being had been a perfect answer to theirs. [P. 95]

Baako has anticipated his loneliness in Ghana. Indeed, he is responsible for the fact that no one greets him in Accra, for he has cut short his planned stopover in Paris on his way home from the United States and has taken the first plane to Accra. The beauty of Paris has proven inaccessible to him; it only intensifies his isolation.

> In the attraction of this beauty itself there was the thing that made enjoyment impossible for him. He had not been able to perceive anything without having it deepen that unsettling feeling that was not only one of loneliness but a much more fearful emotion, as if there never was going to be any way out of his giddying isolation. [P. 78]

Something has occurred to him during his stay abroad that has disengaged him from his countrymen, perhaps from all men. Here is another kind of disorder attendant upon rapid development and Westernization, alienation and strangeness

Thus far, then, Armah has shown the disruptive effects of social change upon family and communal relationships and upon religion. With Baako's return to play the role of alien at home, Armah shows the forces of imbalance at work within the been-to himself as well as in broader communal relationships.

In subsequent chapters, Armah demonstrates similar examples of social and private disorder in Ghanaian society. He intensifies the impact of their presentation by showing their increasingly destructive effects upon Baako, who is already deeply disturbed at the time of his arrival. "Nothing works," his friend Ocran tells him. "The place is run by this so-called elite of pompous asses trained to do nothing" (p. 223). Baako has naively followed the official procedure of filling out papers for the civil service commission in hopes of a position with the national television service. Ocran tells him that his papers will go nowhere unless Baako bribes the clerk to process them or finds some other means to make things happen. Baako is considerably less knowing than the young Elsie Marks, who offers herself to Obi Okonkwo for his aid in securing her a scholarship.

Ocran's influence with the principal secretary of the ministry of information results in Baako's being hired on the spot. Personal influence, not procedure, is what is required among Ghana's miniscule elite, into which Baako is now admitted. The principal secretary remarks, "Unfortunately, . . . the young man will . . . be finding out that making a go of life means forgetting all the beautiful stuff they teach in the class room. It's very different, the way things really work." [P. 124]

The truth of these words is soon manifest to Baako when he presents his television scripts at a production meeting at Ghanavision. His superior, Asante-Smith, rejects Baako's work, despite his care in writing, for it is too idealistically concerned with moral values. Asante-Smith tells him, "You're too abstract in your approach to our work" (p. 212). Ghanavision must use its tape for filming the head of state, his lieutenants, and the events of national holidays. Baako's burning his scripts in dejection after having resigned his job is followed shortly by his second mental collapse. Events have indicated to him that he is an indigenous stranger. The rejection of his work, however, is irrefutable evidence of his alienation. In resigning his job, he at once retains his identity and affirms his alienation, albeit disastrously so.

Another development in the novel indicative of fundamental disorder is the birth and death of Baako's sister's child. The baby is born dangerously early, and the family is caught unawares. Baako rushes his sister, Araba, to the hospital in a taxi. She is rejected at a new maternity ward because neither Baako nor Araba's husband has sufficient rank or prestige. The baby is delivered in an older, less prestigious ward. After the child is born, the mother and grandmother, thoroughly caught up in their passion for goods, think of the material gain it can bring. Only a few days after its birth the ritual ceremony of the baby's "outdooring" is held. The date is chosen because it just follows payday and the guests can be counted on to be generous with their gifts.[43] Despite his misgivings, Baako is persuaded to serve as master of ceremonies for the occasion. Sickened by his mother's flagrant encouragement of their guests to give more money, Baako disrupts the ceremony. He drops an electric fan into a pan in which the money has been collected. There is a great clatter; sparks and paper money fly. The baby screams, and the outdooring ends on a discordant note.

"Everything is wrong now," Naana says forebodingly. The early outdooring ceremony is fatal to the premature baby. Disorder pervades even the mourning, for Baako must seek further false prestige by writing a poem of grief to appear in the newspapers, undersigned by the names and titles of the "chief mourners":

> Mrs. Efua Onipa Certified Teacher
> Radiantway International School.
> Mr. Baako Onipa, BA Senior Officer
> Ghanavision.
> Mr. Kwesi Baiden Technical Staff
> Volta Aluminium Company, Tema. [P. 268].

Another death, that of Skido the lorry driver, dramatizes the counterforces of disruption and coherence at war within the Ghanaian society. Trying to force his truck onto a departing ferry boat, Skido is killed when he jumps from the falling vehicle and is crushed by it underwater. Social and personal disorder cause his death. There is no bridge at this point in the river; the jetty is jammed with waiting trucks. When the ferry arrives, available space is taken by the quickest, most aggressive drivers. Skido, whose truck is loaded with perishable food, has been made desperate by a three-day wait. Stung by the injustice of others, taking his place in line, he makes a fatal error. But Skido's death triggers a spontaneous communal action. Because the public works department has refused to act until the next day, Skido's fellow drivers silently work under oil lamps to tow the truck from the river and bring up the body. Like the rabid dog, Skido has died of a crushed skull. Although this scene evokes the earlier violent death, it is calm and filled with compassion. A grieving woman covers the body, saying simply, "Aah, Skido" (p. 206). In this episode Armah suggests that the tragedy has evoked something of the true nature of the Ghanaian people. As they work together in the dark, they have been freed from the chaotic impulses that have come upon them with Westernization and materialism. Although Armah may indict Africans for their struggles for material goods,[44] in this passage they are depicted as a normally rational, loving people who are only periodically visited by a powerful frenzy. When it passes, peace and cooperation remain.

> The riverside at night was changed completely from what it had been during the daylight. The screeching rush was gone, together with the curses of sweating angry men. A heavy breeze rose off the water, turning the misty drizzle into a fine sporadic spray and finally blowing out the little oil lamps one after the other. There were several people, but there was no noise, except now and then a short word, a request or a reply coming from one of the men. [P. 204]

John Povey cites Armah as "the most distinguished example of the second generation of African writers."[45] The validity of this assertion is evident in Armah's brilliant culminating excoriation of African materialism. In a mood of high intensity, Baako writes in his notebook, hoping to arrive at an integral meaning of his deeply disturbed reactions to his country's social disorder. He compares Africans with their passion for goods to the Melanesians who worship as gods cargo-carrying American airplanes. "So how far, how close are we to Melanesia? It can be seen as a pure rockbottom kind of realism, the approach that accepts what happens at this moment in this place and raises it to the level of principle" (p. 225).

Baako contends that Africans have come to perceive the West in much the same way as the cargo cultists dimly understand it, as the realm of the beyond, the spirit world from which commodity flows. The intermediary between the African and this perversion of the world of the spirits is the been-to. When he returns from the beyond, Baako writes, the been-to fulfills his function by bringing cargo with him or seeing to it that it follows him.

> At any rate, it clearly understood that the been-to has chosen, been awarded, a certain kind of death [in his going abroad]. A beneficial death, since cargo follows his return. Not just cargo, but also importance, power, a radiating influence capable of touching ergo elevating all those who in the first instance have suffered the special bereavement caused by the been-to's going away. [Pp. 225–226]

In this climactic portion of the novel, Armah projects his most vilifying vision of Ghana. In Baako's notes, the fragments of disorder presented earlier in the book cohere in horrifying, mad logic. Given Baako's ironic assumption that commodity has replaced God as the highest good, everything that has gone before makes sense. The disparate examples of social malfunctioning are now apparent as components of an entire system of disorder. Armah has shown us Ghana as a sickened, reverse image of a healthy normal society.

In addition to achieving the highest expression of social realism in *Fragments*, the bitter conceit of the cargo cult also sets forth in dramatic clarity those mythic aspects of the novel which are adumbrated throughout earlier sections.

> He [the been-to] is the ghost in person returned to live among men, a powerful ghost understood to the extent that he behaves like a powerful ghost, cargo and all. . . . In many ways the been-to cum ghost is and has to be a transmission belt for cargo. Not a maker, but an intermediary. Making takes too long, the intermediary brings quick gains. . . . The idea the ghost could be a maker, apart from being too slow-breaking to interest those intent on living as well as the system makes possible, could also have something of excessive pride in it. Maker, artist, but also maker, god. It is presumably a great enough thing for a man to rise to be an intermediary

between other men and the gods. To think of being a maker oneself could be sheer unforgivable sin. . . . Hubris for the Greeks. [Pp. 226–227]

Armah has endowed his protagonist with an artist's sensibility and thus can express the metaphoric truth of Baako's situation without resorting to an intruding authorial voice. The role that Baako sees as his own is nothing short of epic. Since the evidence of his experience has overwhelmingly demonstrated to him that the spirit world of the Ghanaian people has been replaced by the world of commodity as the highest good, all known order is threatened. In the dual chaos of his own madness and the madness of the society around him, Baako is in an unstructured realm, the order of which he must create himself. This restructuring is an epic act: "A victim of irrationality, man sees his peace and fulfillment in control: Against chaos he opposes logos."[46] Baako is in fact two kinds of hero: the realistic hero of the novel tradition and the epic hero of myth. "The tragic and epic artist generalized character by dissociating it from a particular point in time and space, but the novelist individualized character by rendering it as the product of just such a point in time and space."[47]

The particularized character of Baako Onipe serves a much broader purpose than fascinating the reader with admirable traits and an exciting personal history. He epitomizes the been-to; he embodies Africa in this century. He also, however, is a figure who struggles for meaning even though his surroundings have become arbitrary or formless.

Because the social criticism of *Fragments* is so readily apparent in Armah's explicitly descriptive scenes of Ghana of the 1960s, the novel's deeper meanings are perhaps somewhat less so. But a close reading reveals a carefully ordered structure that serves quite another function than simply to advance the narrative.

Fragments is essentially the story of Baako's experience. Yet Armah provides a narrative frame with four chapters employing the points of view of Naana and Juana. Naana's voice opens and closes the novel. Juana's voice follows hers at the beginning and precedes hers at the novel's close. This formal structure of double prologue and epilogue and the selection of Naana's words impart significant tonal qualities to the novel. Through Naana, Armah presents the exposition of the narrative. She remembers Baako's departure, expressing herself with a simple and repetitive formal unworldliness, the ceremonial language of one removed from pragmatic concerns of the contemporary world. "Nothing [of the proper rituals] was left out before he was taken up into the sky to cross the sea and to go past the untouchable horizon itself. . . . Nothing was said then that was not to be said, and nothing remained unsaid for which there was a need" (pp. 14–15).

She is concerned with matters of decorum, order, and the propitiation of the gods to ensure the success of Baako's venture. This sense of order and containment are present in her poetic prayers.

> And when he returns
> let his return, like rain
> bring us your blessings and their fruits
> your blessings
> your help
> in this life you have left us to fight alone.
> With your wisdom
> let him go,
> let him come.
> And you, traveller about to go,
> Go and return
> Go, come. [P. 18]

Naana's perception of Baako's undertaking is also presented in poetic terms: "I saw Baako roaming in the unknown, forbidden places, just born there again after a departure and a death somewhere. He had arrived from beneath the horizon and standing in a large place that was open and filled with many winds, he was lonely" (p. 24).

Thus, it is apparent that the novel opens with a formal tone not generally associated with social realism. In the final chapter poetic aspects of the novel are again apparent. A cycle has been completed. Whereas in the beginning Baako was the traveler in the land beyond the horizon, Naana now sees herself as the traveler: "When there is no use, the spirit in us yearns for the world of other spirits, travellers who have crossed over from this side, just as the spirits themselves hope and wait for the new one coming" (p. 278).

She reviews what has gone before: Baako's arrival, the demands placed on him by his family, the death of the child, Baako's breakdown, and her hope for his recovery and eventual success. She expresses a traditional African view of the cyclical nature of experience. Things have changed; a minimal progress has been achieved, but these developments are all part of the unceasing flow of life of which Naana feels herself to be a part. Convinced, moreover, of an afterlife, she is quite resigned to death.[48] The novel ends ritualistically with her words, "Take me. I am ready. You are the end. The beginning. You who have no end. I am coming" (p. 286).

Naana's final words shift the novel's focus and meaning from that of Baako's experiences in contemporary Ghana. The ending is only generally related to those events. They do not cause it. Her coming death, however, places Baako in a world that has symbolically lost contact with the old order. Thus, the imperative of his quest for new order and meaning is intensified.

Naana's priestlike words are incantatory and benedictive, imparting the quality of ritual to the narrative. As Northrop Frye tells us, in fact, the origin of narrative can be seen in ritual, "a ritual being a temporal sequence of acts in which the conscious meaning or significance is latent; it can be seen by an observer but is largely concealed from the participators themselves."[49] And, further, according to Frye, it is myth that gives the ritual its significance. The carefully structured, organized acts seek a kind of occult efficacy to bring about the proper continuation of mutability.

Although Baako knowingly develops the conceit that expresses the corruption of Ghana's moral values, the novel as a ritual is an expression of Armah's consciousness, not his protagonist's. So it can be said then that Baako is an unknowing celebrant of the ritual that is made up by the total novel. As a mythic hero, he is on the ultimate mythic quest. Again Frye aids our understanding.

> This is the same goal, of course, that the attempt to combine human and natural power in ritual has. The social function of the arts, therefore, seems to be closely connected with visualizing the goal of work in human life. So in terms of significance, the central myth of art must be the vision of the end of social effort, the innocent world of fulfilled desires, the free human society.[50]

This explanation is also an explanation of Baako's trouble. Like "the man" of *The Beautyful Ones Are Not Yet Born*, Baako is distressed by the reality of Ghanaian life because he has a standard, an ideal to which he can compare all that he sees around him. He is not unique to African life, for social consciousness is central to traditional African civilization. Lacking sophisticated means of defense against illness and infirmity, wars, and natural disasters, Africans have become highly skilled at organizing human relationships to facilitate harmony and understanding. The incursion into Africa of Western values, producing growing isolation and even anomy, is detrimental to the achievement in which Africans have perhaps surpassed the West, the highly sophisticated development of man's social nature.[51]

In addition to the narrative structure and Naana's ceremonial language, other elements support the contention that *Fragments* is ritualistic. We have already discussed the ritualistic aspects of the killing of the rabid dog, the death of Skido the truck driver, and the fatal early outdooring of Araba's baby. Not only do they provide evidence of the malfunctioning of those organizations that formerly maintained communal harmony, they also present ritualized patterns of the contending forces for order and disruption. Another highly significant ritual pattern is found in the depiction of sexual harmony between Juana and Baako. Baako's art, as central to his being, and Juana's healing powers, as central to hers, are of major importance to this passage. The myth of the water goddess is repeated in several versions. The first is an example of perverted art. Akosua Russell, a false poet who has pretentions to being the *grande dame* of Ghanaian letters, presents the myth in an execrable poem. Armah employs the sequence to burlesque the poetry of Efua Sutherland, Russell's real-life counterpart.[52] Baako's simple telling of the Myth of Mame Water to Juana is the second version of the myth. A musician plays his guitar and sings so well at the water's edge that a beautiful sea goddess comes to him to make love. He is able to call her up from the sea only at rare intervals, however; when she is gone, he suffers intensely and fears he can never bring her back. He must do so with his art and thus subject himself to continuing tests of his authenticity. The repetition of the myth is suggested in Baako and Juana's sexual acts, some of which occur in or near water. The whole story of their relationship, their separation and reunion, Baako as the artist, Juana, the psychiatrist, as the healing goddess, is still another rendering of the ritual relationship with its mythic overtones.

Just as the elements of social criticism combine in the centrally cohering conceit of Ghana as Melanesia, so too do the novel's varied ritual aspects achieve a transcendent unity—a ritualization of Baako's quest for coherence of the fragments of the old order into a new synthesis.

Chinua Achebe has said that Armah left Ghana for America when he was still "too young." Achebe feels that one result of this early departure was Armah's disengagement of feeling for his home country. According to Achebe, *The Beautyful Ones Are Not Yet Born* and *Fragments* lack compassion. "In places they read almost like the report of a colonial officer" (the Amherst interview). It would not appear, however, that these works, *Fragments* in particular, reflect a lack of feeling for Ghana. On the contrary, Armah's compassion for the plight of Ghanaians is clearly evident. The intensity of the adventures of "the man" and Baako evinces this compassion. The fragmentation of the traditional culture of Ghana or the cultures of Africa at large, while dramatically evident and, for many, personally distressing, is not an isolated cultural phenomenon. *Fragments* is a universally significant novel, an artful expression of the immutable given of human experience—in us and around us, nothing is fixed, everything changes. Chaos is always at hand and must be held in check by the creative, ordering powers of human consciousness.

Through his private vision and the uniqueness of his art, the novelist exhibits reality and, in a limited way, creates reality. The aim of his investigation of experiences is not to plumb a depth to find only an objective, forced, unyielding central core of truth, but ultimately to discover what other possible modes of being lie in human consciousness. The lyric qualities of the three novels we have just considered demonstrate the capacity of the genre to reveal these private visions of reality. For even though Laye and Kane and Armah carry us far beyond the immediate facts of contemporary Africa, their novels take their departure from the most basic facts of African reality. In *The Life of the Novel*, David Goldknopf rightly points out that

> the primary, in fact, the all-embracing, interest of the novel is realism: the historical commission of the novel, which came into existence as a record of the mind's circulation through the world as-it-is. Realism is the generic commitment of the novel, its contract with the reader. In a responsible novel it is a contract to repay that attention with the illumination of reality that is the novel's wisdom.[53]

Yet, tempered by our common perceptions of the real, the novelist's private vision, in turn, gives our sense of reality new form. "The art of the novel is finally, by tradition and generic commitment, realistic. We must trust the novel because it has nowhere to hide; it works in the openness of its realism."[54] But of experience comes idea, and idea, in turn, continually reshapes the facts of experience, clarifying, giving new meaning and pointing to new possibilities. And through art, slow, historical incremental change at intervals leaps into exponential growth. Such mythic figures as Samba Diallo, Clarence, and Baako reflect the artists' responses to the slow accumulation of ideas. They have presented us new whole visions out of the fragments of their experiences.

John Povey writes,

> Armah must be considered the most distinguished example of the second generation of African writers. His work, although highly individual, may be evidence of the direction the African novel will take in the next few years. Because he has written several works it is possible to trace a developing philosophy. It is not a new negritude. It is not a shallow call for administrative reform. It is not even absolutely a denunciation of colonialism. It looks inward into the spiritual malaise in Africa today from which all the merely surface evidence of corruption and exploitation derive. Armah is not a satirist pricking small balloons of folly and illusion that exist around the fringes of a generally tolerated system that has merely foibles to correct. His is a moralist's denunciation, inspired by the frenzy of a high rage.[55]

Povey's assessment of Armah's rank in African letters is accurate. But Armah and Kane and Laye must be seen as more than moral philosophers. For *Fragments* and *The Radiance of the King* and *Ambiguous Adventure* are also adventures of a special sort, for their creators and for their readers as well. Each work takes us to a moment of high illumination when " 'things' are freed from their time bound existence."[56]

These three works earn Armah, Laye, and Kane high honors indeed. They have affirmed a powerful tendency of the novel to link together realism and individualism and have shown a mode of carrying individualism through art to its highest form.

Although the issue of the been-to experience was a fruitful source for exciting literature from the 1920s to the 1960s, it is not wholly a timeless theme. True, some aspects of the convention, as we have seen, reflect enduring human truths. But one focus of the convention is the depth of meaning of a particular historical truth; hence, it is somewhat limited by history. By the mid-1960s, the vitality of the convention began to wane. New versions of the been-to novel are marked by repetition of the now too-familiar theme or weakened by overelaborate variations upon the theme. Moreover, West African realities are changing. Been-tos no longer experience the privileges or the discomforts of extraordinary persons. They are now too numerous; furthermore, they must compete for prestige with the graduates of indigenous universities. These factors have their effects upon the convention. Nonetheless, the theme remains capable of expressing important human truths. We shall see in the next chapter how for a time the convention is treated as a mere cliché but how later, even in flawed works, it demonstrates its continued significance.

Chapter Four

New Treatments of the Been-to Convention

During the past ten years, the convention of the been-to in West African fiction has undergone significant changes. The power that the convention imparts to *Ambiguous Adventure*, for example, seems to be waning. Frequent repetition produces contrivance and predictability. Although Armah's highly successful *Fragments* was yet to come, the static qualities of the convention are apparent in the other work produced by the mid-sixties, even in the novels that attempt to make major variations upon the form. All too often, the been-to convention restates the same case and voices the same complaints: Africa is not as it was; the West has poisoned us all; corruption is widespread; the old center does not hold; things, particularly the been-to, fragment. Yet even though the convention is often treated as a cliché during the period, the theme remains valid.

It also happens that many of the novels that employ the convention from the mid-1960s on are, in various ways, technically weak. These technical weaknesses, significant though they may be, do not account for the diminishing effectiveness of the convention during this time. That development is simply owing to the fact that the convention is going through a period of stereotyped uses. Its potential in the hands of accomplished writers is still great. The exact nature of the relationship, whether temporal or causal, between the flaws of these novels and the apparent diminishing effectiveness of the convention is beyond the limits of this study. It is important, however, to note that during the 1960s and the early 1970s, the convention was employed by leading West African writers in works that are often seriously flawed. As we shall see, the disunity of Soyinka's novel *The Interpreters* demonstrates all too clearly that Nigeria's greatest playwright was but a fledgling novelist at the time of its writing. Furthermore, *A Dream of Africa* shows none of the coherence and control that marks Laye's earlier novels. *This Earth, My Brother,* among its other flaws, exhibits the very symptoms of the been-to neurosis as it confusingly echoes Western literatures. Kole Omotoso's book *The Edifice* is a very slight novella, but its substance requires an extended novel for full development. Armah's *Why Are We So Blest?* is thesis ridden, its characters constrained to demonstrate the novelist's point.

Nevertheless, to point out the need for distinction between the technical flaws of the works and the treatment of the convention as a cliché, we should note that the last two works, their flaws notwithstanding, clearly indicate their authors' conscious rejection of the conventional heroic role of the been-to. In this present chapter, I shall attempt to set forth these developments in the convention, first by discussing what have become the standard characteristics of the convention, then by analyzing the novels listed above. First, let us consider those shared traits of the been-to convention which were already clearly discernible by the mid-1960s.

A primary trait of the convention is the theme of social disorder. Brempong's consuming materialism has its counterparts in several West African works of fiction. As we have seen, *No Longer at Ease* presents examples ranging from minor to major of the corruption that plagues modern Nigeria. A similar index of social disorder appears in Amma Atta Aidoo's short story "Everything Counts." She focuses her attention upon the popularity of the wearing of wigs of European hair by the urban women of Ghana. Aidoo employs the device as a symbol of the Ghanaian internalization of European values. The short story ends with a hint of an even more advanced stage of cultural decline. The woman chosen to represent the country in the Miss Earth contest is a light-skinned mulatto whose natural hair is like that of the wigs that the author deplores.

Wole Soyinka's *Interpreters* depicts a group of young been-tos all of whom become deeply cynical of the corruption, hypocrisy, and ludicrous aping of European ways which they encounter upon their return to Nigeria. T. M. Aluko's comic *Kinsman and Foreman* tells of a been-to trained as an engineer who must deal with the shady morals and outright dishonesty of his relatives, who exploit the young man's new government position in very innovative ways. The theme of Gabriel Okara's novel *The Voice* fits within the been-to convention. The protagonist returns to his village from a Western education, which he has received in his own country. Though he does not return from abroad, he is very like his literary counterparts who do. He attacks the moral sterility of his culture and the ways of his elders. He eventually becomes so disruptive and threatening that he is put to death. Thus, these novels, like the others we have already examined, deliberately use the convention as a means for social criticism. In fact, this is one of its most prominent uses.

Another standard theme of the convention is the crisis of the end of youth. As the been-to seeks to enter the adult world of his nation where academic truths must be reconciled to practical needs and to the facts of human failure or greed, he must confront the hard task of converting his dreams into something that fits into contemporary West African reality. Fatoman of Laye's *Dream of Africa* returns to Guinea after six years of study in Paris, convinced that he is inadequately prepared for life as an adult and a professional. The five protagonists of Soyinka's *Interpreters*, with European or American memories fresh in their minds, have just entered their professions or are in the process of doing so. Obi Okonkwo never quite gets into stride with the demands of his new social and professional status. Jeffery Ummuma of Samuel Ifejika's story "The Malaise of Youth" has just returned to his country, Buwono, and must choose which of two offers he will accept, to be the chairman of the National Committee for Development Planning or a professor of economics. Gabriel Okara's protagonist in *The Voice* is a recent returnee whose search for the ineffable "It" has just begun. (As we shall see, Ammamu of *This Earth, My Brother* by Kofi Awoonor, even though very much the been-to and continually remembering the fact, is something of an exception to this pattern. He is older than his literary counterparts and is an attorney with an established career.) Modin, Armah's protagonist in *Why Are We So Blest?* is still a student, distressed that what will await him after his degree and his return to Africa will be an unchallenging life of mediocrity. When Samba Diallo returns to Senegal, he is still young but already haunted by a curse of spiritual impotence. Sissie of Amma Atta Aidoo's short story "Everything Counts" is just beginning her career as a lecturer in economics. When the principal secretary tells Baako that he will soon learn that what he has been taught is very different from the realities of the world, he cites a lesson that many a been-to undergoes. The convention typically presents the protagonist painfully learning how much is involved in the launching of his career.

In a stylized manner, then, the convention often presents the protagonist as eager to become a part of his society but increasingly aware of the dangers it presents. Affected by what he has experienced abroad, inexperienced in the adult world, especially the unfamiliar new Africa, the been-to becomes caught in a series of difficulties. The outcome is often disastrous.

Another frequently repeated characteristic is the protagonist's deep loneliness. Often, remembering his isolation abroad, he is equally lonely at home. For example, Doumbé of *A Few Nights and Days* by Mbella Dipoko longingly remembers his home while he chats with Thérèse, his Parisienne mistress.

> Being a geography student, she would have talked to me about the regions of Europe; about the rivers, for example. But . . . I didn't care for any river but Mungo River in Cameroon, and about that I talked. . . . My childhood by that river. River of desire. River of love songs . . . welcoming river.[1]

But Paris, even while Thérèse waits in his bed, fills him with loneliness. "The sky leaned over Paris. Looking at it, I felt alone, profoundly alone."[2] Modin of *Why Are We So Blest?* writes in his journal:

> The search for knowledge should not be synonymous with increasing alienation and loneliness. In our particular circumstances it is so. It has been planned that way. Knowledge about the world we live in is the property of the alien because the alien has conquered us. The thirst for knowledge therefore becomes perverted into a desire for getting close to the alien, getting out of the self. Result: loneliness is a way of life.[3]

And Ammamu of *This Earth, My Brother*, moving through the events of the novel in chilled, neurotic isolation, incapable of close contact with his family or friends, even in his elitist club, thinks of his earlier isolation during his university days: "We, the best of nature's freaks, African intellectuals, are returning from Oxford."[4] And earlier in the novel: "He drove away, not having said a word to anyone. By now they would be discussing him. That he was a funny man" (pp. 136–137). Similarly, Samba Diallo's conviction that he is the only human among a tide of moving automatons along the Boulevard St. Michel expresses a sense of isolation that was later to be tiresomely repeated in other works. Obi Okonkwo's ruin derives largely from the isolation into which his financial problems have forced him. He can explain to no one, not even Clara, his fiancée, the real depth of the trap in which he finds himself. And when Fatoman in Laye's *A Dream of Africa* tells Marie regarding Paris, "It's very cold over there, so cold, that living here, you can't possibly imagine what it is like," he is not merely referring to the climate, but to the chill of the isolation he has experienced there as well.[5]

Consistent with the themes of alienation and disorder in the been-to theme is the disastrous outcome for the protagonist. As we shall see, Modin of *Why Are We So Blest?* dies a brutal death at the hands of racist French colons. Okolo of *The Voice* is tied back to back to Tuere, a supposed witch who has befriended him, and set adrift in a canoe to drown in a whirlpool. Samba Diallo dies; Obi Okonkwo goes to prison. Ammamu of *This Earth, My Brother* and Baako go mad. The pull of two worlds, seemingly admitting of no synthesis, is too demanding for the been-to to survive the psychic wound he has suffered.

Contemporary West African reality undoubtedly imposes many similar kinds of experiences upon been-tos. Nevertheless, one wonders if many of the similarities of been-to novels derive from the influence of the convention, rather than from life itself. In fact, the protagonists of many been-to novels appear to act as they do because of the requirements of the convention rather than because of internal motivation. For example, we do not see Ammamu's motivation. Nothing accounts for his madness in a specific way. We see results of various stages of the changes he undergoes, but nothing accounts for the details of the change. There is no suggestion of his having a character flaw, only a finely honed sensibility that suffers from the inadequacies of others. What is wrong with Okolo? Why is he seeking the mysterious "It"? Does his quest drive him mad, or is it merely a symptom of a madness whose existence we are required to accept? One need not know the hero's every passing thought, but the basis for his motivation should be clear. The cool, Joycean posture of Sagoe of *The Interpreters*, who sees himself as an alien in a wasteland, is very much like Ammamu's, whose posture is like that of Baako, who in turn reminds us of Obi.

Although the similarity of Baako's attitudes to those of Obi does not hinder the success of *Fragments*, we can note here the beginnings of a trait that will become tiresome in later works. Therefore, let us turn now from this general view of the convention to closer examination of some later novels that treat this theme of the Western scar.

The Interpreters:
Ethical Discontinuity in Nigeria

With a reputation built upon fourteen plays and a volume of poetry, Wole Soyinka was well established as one of Africa's leading writers when he published his first novel, *The Interpreters*, in 1965. The convention of the been-to is centrally represented in this work, for all of the "interpreters" are been-tos and the major devices of the convention are evident. However, although Soyinka's technique of interrelating the experiences of six been-tos is a significant innovation within the convention, the potential effectiveness of the novel is diminished by flaws in the author's craft.

The bulk of the novel is a series of bright conversations among six young men who have recently returned from the West to begin their careers. These young men—Sagoe, a journalist, Bandele and Kola, university lecturers; Egbo, who serves in the foreign office; Sekoni, an engineer and sculptor; and Lasunwon, a lawyer—are all undergoing a kind of awakening generally characteristic of the been-to convention. In various encounters, they all come to see the solidly structured corruption of their elders and the artful hypocrisy that presents itself to the world as conventional morality.[6]

As we shall see, the novel is difficult to perceive as an entity because Soyinka seems unable to judge to what extent his readers can follow him. Yet there is no obscurity in the novel's central theme, the revelation to the young professionals of the moral disease that affects the elders of their class. In fact, the theme is inescapable, if not belabored. The novel posits two sorts of characters, those who have bought their success at the cost of moral corruption and the youthful, judging "interpreters." The hostility between them is unremitting; there is no hope of reconciliation. The marginal people see the successful Nigerians as hypocrites; they in turn see the young been-tos as irreverent.[7] But Soyinka clearly overstates his case. The dignified judge, Sir Derinola, who had been photographed in a top hat as he walked through St. James Park on his way to be knighted by the queen, is revealed as a hypocrite by Sagoe. The episode is hardly credible, for it is very unlikely that such a man would risk his reputation as

Soyinka has him do. The judge sends one of his underlings into a hotel to receive a bribe for him. Impatient at the long wait for the man's return, the judge enters the hotel and peeps through the fronds of a potted palm into the dining room where the payment is to be made. Sagoe confronts him.

> And Sagoe was never never to forget that look upon his face. Beside the fright and his affronted dignity was marked the anguish of indecision. . . . Sir Derinola was truly paralysed at the confrontation of a future image. . . . Now he saw Sagoe move forward and tried to shrink back behind the palm. They gazed into each other, all subterfuge pointless. It was Sagoe who took his eyes away.[8]

The young been-to, true to the convention, catches out the real culprit who hides behind the dignity of his robes, titles, and office. Sagoe also attacks the falsity of newly appointed Professor Oguazor, whose cultivated Oxbridge accent is as artificial as the plastic flowers and fruits that decorate his house: "Ceroline der, the ledies herv been wetting for you" (p. 153).

Sagoe arouses the displeasure of the socially mobile new professor and his wife by appearing without a tie at the celebration at their house. We are reminded of Obi Okonkwo in *No Longer at Ease*, who was taught a similar lesson when he too evoked the displeasure of the tribal elders by his casual dress. When the professor's wife says of Sagoe, "He is not yet used to things here," she echoes the words directed to other been-tos (ibid.). Obi's friend Joseph grows desperate in his attempts to counsel Obi, as does his father in quite another way. In *Fragments*, the principal secretary says that Baako will soon learn the sharp difference between the ideals taught in the classroom and the ways of the real world. Like Obi and Baako, Sagoe and his friends are unwilling to accept such earnestly offered lessons. Sagoe is compelled to protest the artificiality he finds on the Lagos campus by sniffing the plastic rose worn by Mrs. Oguazor and by pitching their plastic fruit out of the window. This episode demonstrates all too simplistically the virtue of youth and the corruption of their elders. Nothing in the scene suggests that Soyinka is in any way unsympathetic to Sagoe. Only our admiration is called for. Oguazor, like Sir Derinola, is to be seen wholly negatively, he as a fool, Sir Derinola as a villain. Soyinka gives no sense that they are mere weaklings caught up in the world with its human flaws.

Another episode similarly depicts the moral differences between the young and the old. Sekoni's first engineering project is a rural power station that he constructs without knowing that a civil service officer has actually "contracted" the project to a subsidiary company registered in the name of his infant niece. When the public works officials set out to write off the plant as unsafe without ever putting it into operation, Sekoni collapses trying to prove that the plant is actually operative. Like Baako and Ammamu, he spends time in a mental hospital. Then, as been-to heroes often do, he quits his job. Sagoe learns of the complicated network of Nigerian corruption when he tries to expose the episode in a Lagos newspaper. The story will not be published because unrevealed, the information is power that can prevent exposure of the crimes of the publishers of the newspaper. "Everyone, it appears, has something on someone else and the result is that the general public never learns the truth about anything."[9]

Such revelations of the world's corruptions are, of course, standard fare for Künstlerroman in general and for been-to novels in particular. Yet, whereas the subject may be familiar, its mode of presentation is not. Although Soyinka clearly merits high respect for his drama and his poetry, *The Interpreters* is seriously flawed by unsuccessful techniques. Eldred Jones detects characteristic skills carefully developed for other genre also at work in the novel. From his poetry, Jones believes, Soyinka draws his "cryptic, image-laden style"; from his drama, a sense of setting and character; and from his essays, "a fluency of exposition and critical observation."[10] It may well be said that Jones's distinctions are somewhat too fine. In fact, that very virtuosity and those skillful techniques that elicit such general praise for Soyinka's other work do not serve him well in *The Interpreters*. On the contrary, Soyinka's dexterity, when applied to the writing of the novel, changes, like a forest creature in one of his plays, to a demon of uncontrollable powers. Between the constantly shifting point of view and the time jumping back and forth from flashback to slice of the future, the narrative line of *The Interpreters* is almost too complex for comprehension. Although it might be argued that Soyinka has deliberately striven for this effect, this mosaic of impressions is not adequate to convey the psychological and sociological content of the experience of the been-to. In any case, as I shall demonstrate, the techniques that may have lent themselves so well to his plays and lyric poetry prove to be markedly insufficient to the novel, particularly since *The Interpreters* has no real plot. So the eagerly received first novel of Africa's greatest playwright proved to fall far short of what Soyinka's readers had learned to expect of him. The very complexity by which Soyinka demonstrates a myriad of writing talents actually becomes an impediment. Too complex to provide a clearly perceived single experience, *The Interpreters* is a kind of compartmentalized showcase for the writer's skills.

The novel begins *in medias res* in a night club. Sagoe, Bandele, Egbo, and a young woman, Dehinwa, dodge the drips that leak through the roof as a tropical shower suddenly hits. Egbo suddenly says aloud to no one, "Well, I made a choice. I can't complain." Then he explains, "Oh, I was only having a chat with me and this talkative puddle" (p. 4). The scene immediately shifts to a larger body of water. Egbo is in a canoe. The paddlers have brought it to rest against a cannon that sits rusting in the river. He explains to Bandele and Kola that his parents drowned at this spot.

The two scenes are logically linked by the image of water. But there is little beyond that to clarify the purpose of long deviation from the scene in the narrative present. The opening scene has hardly been established before Soyinka shifts our attention elsewhere. Such is the pattern throughout the novel. While Eldred Jones praises Soyinka's use of this shifting focus as a device that provides structural compactness and a "feeling of wholeness of conception," he also acknowledges the difficulties of this technique.[11] Charles R. Larson carefully traces the narrative line of the novel in *The Emergence of African Fiction*. But he also notes that

> in many ways [the narrative line] is the least significant aspect of his novel—that is, for what happens or does not happen to his characters. Technically, the structure is something altogether different from that of any previous African novels. . . . At times this obscurity is more harmful than beneficial to the novel itself and it becomes extremely difficult to grasp Soyinka's meaning. Time is obscured almost completely except for occasional references to specific blocks of time usually between chapters. The flashbacks are often spatial instead of temporal, and the imagery has a tendency to cluster around one given character but to overlap upon others.[12]

Soyinka's statement of the complex interwovenness of Nigerian corruption notwithstanding, the central statement of the novel is a fairly simple one of guilt and condemnation. At the novel's end, the situation is static. The author's protests seem to fall on the empty air. The characters' experiences have not brought them any new understanding. The view of the world that is implicit at the novel's beginning obtains at its end. The reader tires of seeing the old boys and their corrupt apprentices continually shown up, and Soyinka's "verbal dexterity and linguistic sophistication" lead to a general "tedious formlessness."[13]

Despite its shortcomings, *The Interpreters* cannot be written off like Sekoni's power station with charges of "wasteful expenditure," "unsuitable materials," and "[unsafety of] operation" (p. 26). It contains many effective, even brillant, scenes. The central problem of the work may reflect one of the problems of the relationship between life and art. For even though the difficulties of been-tos were still deeply felt in Nigeria in 1965, they had been presented so often in literature that Soyinka perhaps felt that he could not use the convention in a simple, straightforward manner. Consequently, despite his commendable efforts and occasional successes, *The Interpreters* is a seriously flawed novel. Moreover, its often mannered, repetitive restatement of the old story constitutes a stage in the weakening of the literary convention.

A Dream of Africa:
Political Oppression and Literary Disorder

A Dream of Africa, Camara Laye's third novel, is, like his first, an autobiographical work. However, unlike the first, this novel is seriously flawed by inconsistency and disunity. These flaws perhaps reflect some of the difficulties he was experiencing as a been-to, the very same kind of problems that are typically treated by the literary convention. Laye has described *A Dream of Africa* as "une experience un peu rapide," a rapidly written experimental novel, "un roman concret" (the Dakar interview). He asserts that in addition to treating the difficulties of African students in Paris, the novel recounts how his own life "était un peu difficile, mais quand même, je l'ai surmonteé" (ibid.). Indeed, while *A Dream of Africa* does not touch upon the matter directly, it was written during the period of his unhappy career in Guinean politics. Appointed by Sékou Touré to diplomatic posts in neighboring Liberia and Ghana, and later serving as director of the Centre de Recherche in the ministry of information, Laye had had a first-hand view of just how poorly Africans in power were serving the dreams of independence. His withdrawal from the corruption and the profiteering of the new Africans, whom he found as exploitative as their former colonial masters, made him suspect in their eyes. His exile to Senegal subsequently began in 1964. The novel, repressed for political reasons in manuscript form from 1963, was finally published in Paris as Dramouss in 1966.[14]

The novel is dedicated "to the young people of Africa," especially to Laye's fellow been-tos who have returned, often "unprovided with the full armory of modern equipment they had dreamed of bringing back with them . . . not just as an example, but rather as a basis for objective criticism which shall be of profit to our young people and to the future of our Native Land" (p. 7). His intent is to encourage the young to speak out "in the long process of the total restoration of our native ways of thinking [which] in order to resist the ravages of time and temporary fashion, must draw their essential force from historical truths of our respective civilizations and in African realities" (p. 8).

The theme of the work, as the dedication suggests, is based on the protagonist's reactions to his homeland, Guinea, as he finds it after an absence of six years' study in Paris. *A Dream of Africa* is linked with Laye's first novel, *The Dark Child*, not only chronologically but also, as Emile Snyder writes,

> because it represents the hopes of a young man who left for France in order to acquire an education, returned to put this education to a useful task for his country's need and discovered then another side to the coin of independence. If *The Dark Child* evoked the memory of a maternal Africa, open to love and the sense of mystery, *A Dream of Africa* sketches the painful journey from ideal to reality, from the warm meaningful life of Kouroussa to the slum suburbs of Conakry where poverty was as common as dirt.[15]

As Fatoman travels about Guinea, he encounters several indications of Guinea's decline toward social disaster. His boyhood friend Bilali has become a prosperous diamond merchant, passionately absorbed in piling up a fortune and putting it on show. Another friend, the teacher Konaté, is bitterly cynical about the continuing ineffectiveness of Guinea's educational system. The traditional craftsmen in the marketplace are going broke, their customers drawn by mass-produced trinkets imported by Lebanese tradesmen. Fatoman's father, the once powerful magician-goldsmith of *The Dark Child*, complains of the failing efficacy of the traditional gods and looks for the coming of a powerful leader who will save the New Africa. Most serious of all national ills that Fatoman learns of, however, is the failure of politics. The promises of independence are

99

woefully unfulfilled and an incipient totalitarian system is steadily increasing in strength. After a local political meeting Fatoman tells his friends:

> I don't know. All I know is that one day someone must attack all those lies. Someone must say that though colonialism, vilified by that committee, was an evil thing for our country, the regime you are now introducing will be a catastrophe whose evil consequences will be felt for decades. Someone must speak out and say that a regime built on spilt blood through the activities of incendiaries of huts and houses is nothing but a regime of anarchy and dictatorship, a regime based on violence. Some one must shout: "Long live liberty"; but it must not be forgotten that the deputy elected to the French Government by this country, and who has just voted at the Palais-Bourbon for the suppression of the Algerian freedom movement has acted like a neo-colonialist. At the same time, our closest neighbor, Senegal, governed by a deputy who is also a poet, had taken a stand against the war in Algiers. That's what I call realism! . . . Someone must say that you have already betrayed the R.D.A. and, at the same time, the great humanist who was its founder. Someone must say that the violence you are now bringing into being in this land will be paid for by each one of you, and especially by the innocent. Above all, in order to establish a workable social system, there must be more concrete action, honest activity, and less speechifying; more respect for the opinions of others, more brotherly love. [Pp. 146–7]

After he separates from his friends, Fatoman, fully aware that he has expressed the most idealistic of hopes, ruminates on his situation. His complaint is a familiar one.

> Strangely enough, I had never until that evening felt and understood the divided nature of my being. My being, I now realized, was compounded of two inner "me's": the first, closer to my own feeling for life, fashioned by my traditional animist background, faintly tinctured with Islamism and enriched by French culture, fought against the second, a personage who, out of love for his native land, was going to betray his true ideas by coming back to live in this new regime. A regime which would also, without any doubt whatsoever, betray at one and the same time, socialism, capitalism, and the African tradition. This kind of bastard regime now in process of formation, after using the Church, the Mosque and Fetishism for support, would after its triumph, deny God. It had already destroyed democracy after the advent of the "loi Deferre," and begun to muzzle the innocent population of Guinea. In the future, it would transform our churches and our

mosques into nightclubs, our sacred forests into places for theatrical spectacles. Thence arose the justified anger of Issa and of his brother the Prophet, demanding justice from the All High; thence arose, too, the lamentations that the virgin forests chanted to the gods. We were threatened by the vengeance of heaven. Thence the gradual degeneration of our native arts and social life, thence the frenzied brayings I had just had to listen to, and those madhouse screamings by which it was claimed we were constructing a society that asks only to eat and live in peace . . . I had been walking straight ahead, and, without realizing it, had reached my home. The conflict between the two "me's"—or rather, my helplessness in the conflict between these two "me's"—was such that I could not eat. [Pp. 147–48]

Fatoman seems to see his personal division as rather more simple than he actually describes it. The "first self," the one he has grown more comfortable with, is shaped by the influences of three cultures, traditional African, Islam, and French. The "second self" seems actually to be more accurately designated as primary, the Guinean, who, despite all other influences or the current political regime, loves his native land and must be there. Those distinctions notwithstanding, Fatoman is still another divided been-to.

The problem with *A Dream of Africa* is not merely that the convention has been so often used. The effectiveness of the novel is also diminished because it is poorly written. Let us now consider the second of these weaknesses.

A Dream of Africa, autobiographical and bearing witness to its author's self-division, lacks unity. The story line, sequential rather than causally developmental, runs as follows. After six years' absence in France, Fatoman returns to see his family. Stopping first in Conakry at the home of his uncle, he learns that his marriage to Marie, his childhood sweetheart, has been formalized in Islamic rituals. The two slowly get to know each other again as they tour the city of Conakry, and Marie tells of her troubles during their long separation. Then they travel to Fatoman's home village of Kouroussa in the highlands, the setting of much of *The Dark Child*. A flashback follows that tells of his difficulties in Paris, his romance with Françoise, a serious illness, and his decision to return (briefly) to Guinea. He meets his old friends, Bilali and Konaté, with whom he discusses politics, next attends a political meeting, and then discusses with his father Guinea's worsening political and economic developments. That night he sleeps with a magic cowrie-shell-covered ball under his pillow, a talisman given to him by his father to inspire dreams of Guinea's future. Fatoman dreams of a fearful, irrational totalitarian state, a Guinea terrorized by the "Big Brute." His vision extends to a later period when Guinea has been saved by the coming of a heroic leader. "I gazed upon my Guinea, guided with wisdom by the Black Lion, the heroic and wise Black Lion" (p. 179).

Fatoman awakens to discover that the hut is afire. The damage is not serious. His father explains that the fire was caused by Dramouss, an extraordinarily beautiful woman of mysterious powers who appeared in Fatoman's dream. Fatoman's father apologizes for not having warned his son against sleeping with Marie, his bride. Dramouss, he claims, has set the fire in a jealous rage. Shortly thereafter, Fatoman and Marie leave Guinea for Paris, where they stay for some years. When they return with their growing family, Fatoman's father tells him that the totalitarian state decreed by Dramouss is now an actuality. Repression is widespread; Fatoman's friends Bilali and Konaté have been killed; others are in prison or exile. The father's report and the novel end with the affirmation of his conviction of the return of law and justice with the coming of the "heroic and infinitely wise" Black Lion, the political saviour (p. 189).

Although a chronological coherence provides a semblance of unity, the incidents of the work primarily serve to set forth its political commentary. The character of the protagonist and the immediacy of his personal responses are clearly secondary. Whereas the incidents that might occasion a course of deeply felt changes are present in the work, they do not lead to a unified and coherent experience, such as one undergoes reading *The Dark Child* or *The Radiance of the King*. Laye has not adapted his material to his form. Fatoman, while concerned about Guinean politics to the point of preoccupation, is not a political person. Although he has strong opinions, he does not speak at the political meeting even though the audience is clearly ready to hear from him. In the dream sequence, he is a passive, bewildered prisoner; moreover, what he experiences *is* only a dream. When he returns to the country years later, the totalitarian regime is in power. He has neither hindered nor helped its coming. The focus of the novel is politics, but politics in no way materially affects the course of Fatoman's life. Nor do the other passages, the romance in Paris, or the tale of the jealous husband have any bearing upon the protagonist's concerns for his nation.

In contrast to the reservations expressed here, O. R. Dathorne describes *Dramouss* (*A Dream of Africa*) as "perhaps Laye's best novel so far."[16] He praises the novel's symbolism and poetry and the forthrightness of its political expression. Although the work is commendable for its instances of poetry and its compelling symbolism and although Laye is to be admired for the incisive and courageous political commentary in the work, these elements alone or in concert do not make for great literature. Laye's own discomfiture with the novel is evident. Asked if *A Dream of Africa* were an experimental novel, Laye responded,

> Oui, oui, oui, c'est quelque chose de réalisme . . . de trés contraire; alors, on ne peut pas faire ce que l'on veut, si on veut étre fidèle dans le developpement des réalitiés, tandis qu'un roman, comme mon *Regard du roi*, on a plus de plaisir, on a plus de charme, d'imagination, qu'un roman comme celui-la, qui était un roman concret, une autobiographie aussi, mais une autobiographie très distincte. [The Dakar interview]
>
> "Yes. Yes. Yes. It is something of realism, very much against the grain; one cannot do what he wants, even if he wants to be faithful to the development of real events. While for a novel like my [Radiance of the King] one has more pleasure, has more charm than [derives from] a novel like that one, which was a concrete novel, an autobiography also, but a very distinct autobiography."

That art and autobiography are often joined in uneasy union is well known. The urgency to tell what happened may well run counter to the requirements of art; even though Laye may have told us what happened, the artistic weakness of *A Dream of Africa* is its form. Although Alain Robbe-Grillet cautions, "A new form will always seem more or less an absence of any form at all, since it is judged by references to the consecrated forms,"[17] a novel must assert its form in such a way that the reader responds to it as an entity. Lacking an organic plot and shifting in emphasis and point of view, *A Dream of Africa* fails to take on a shape that conveys any clear meaning.

Laye's failure to exploit the novel's clear potential is curious, given his demonstrated abilities in *The Dark Child* and *The Radiance of the King*. His materials would seem to lend themselves to a structured form very easily. The young man gradually experiences the world's coming in at him. Relations with Françoise and Marie teach him of the responsibility for the emotional needs of others, the limits of choice he must face up to. In Guinea, he learns of still wider responsibilities—marriage, parenthood, and the claims of responsible citizenship even at the risk of personal danger. The elements are here, but a governing form is not.

The Western Scar

Although the novel's success is greatly diminished by its aesthetic weakness—its commendable defense of political freedom notwithstanding—it is clear that once again Laye has focused upon the man of two worlds. And, in fact, Fatoman, in stating his own divisions, may well suggest the cause of Laye's failure in this work: the lack of a dynamic link between the novel's two main issues—the dominant political criticism and Fatoman's quiet readying of himself to take up life under the repressive regime. Laye does not develop this point very incisively. But, as is the case with many other literary been-tos, Fatoman's division, his European and African identities, have produced an almost paralyzing war within him.

In Laye's three works, the theme of the been-to is eminently present in one form or another. For better or worse, Camara Laye, like so many other West African writers, considered it a given that the sensibilities of his protagonists are powerfully affected by the divisiveness of the claims of two cultures. For Clarence of *The Radiance of the King*, Fatoman, and his unnamed youthful counterpart of *The Dark Child*, it is the West that is the source of a psychic wound; and the healing that nonetheless leaves a scar must derive from a reassertion of Africanness. The convention is repeated frequently because so many young African elites have undergone the experience and struggled to retain their African identities. In fact, the painful struggle seems for some young Africans to have become synonymous with the sign of future success.

But the frequent repetition of the theme need not, in itself, be tantamount to illegitimacy. On the contrary, as I hope I have demonstrated, the weaknesses of *A Dream of Africa* lie in other matters, not in the use of the convention itself. Nevertheless, it is clear that by the mid-1960s, there was a need for the convention to be used with some ingenuity for continued significance and freshness. Laye's failure to exploit the theme fully as a vehicle for presenting the Guinean situation makes it clear that the use of the theme alone no longer carried sufficient impact to produce an effective novel.

This Earth, My Brother:
A Known Story

By the end of the decade, the declining power of the convention of the been-to seems to have compelled other novelists to resort to other literary embellishments to augment the failing appeal of the old story. The following description of Kofi Awoonor's *This Earth, My Brother*, a novel published in 1971, indicates just how familiar the details of the convention have become:

> Kofi Awoonor's only novel . . . describes the plight of Ammamu, a Ghanaian lawyer who returns home from England only to find that the Africa he once knew has drastically changed. He takes refuge in nostalgia and finally drowns himself. [Awoonor, while somewhat equivocal in his language, nevertheless does not suggest that Ammamu drowns himself. He goes mad and is found on the beach. The final chapter presents his parents' arrival at the madhouse to pick up Ammamu's effects. There, his death is alluded to, all indications being that he has died in the insane asylum. Of what is not made clear. A broken heart? Westernness?] Awoonor intends this tale to have symbolical ramifications for all Africa and to some extent he does succeed. Certain poetical devices—references to the sea for instance—are used and work beautifully. The book is a poet's novel and, at times, Awoonor's language is the language of poetry gone sour, not the language of prose. Nevertheless reinforced by rich imagery, the novel does succeed in showing that Ammamu's breakdown represents the obvious collapse of a legacy of colonialism and the corrupt influences of the present.[18]

Once again we have the known formula. Despite Awoonor's attempts to enliven the story by the uniqueness of his style, it remains quite apparent that he is merely retelling the old story. *This Earth, My Brother* is a further example of the decline of the convention. It clearly demonstrates how the divided been-to has by now become a boringly repetitive device. Moreover, Awoonor's taste and judgment repeatedly fail throughout the novel. The result is a tired convention burdened by an overly ambitious style.

In *The Novel and Reality in Africa and America*, Professor Michael Echeruo implies that *This Earth, My Brother* fails because Africa has changed.

> I do not think it will be right to use that term ["moral passion"] to describe Awoonor in *This Earth, My Brother* and quite a lot of other novels that show the same interest, the same commitment, but lack, if you like, the achievement that comes with passion. . . . I am saying this quite advisedly because it is difficult . . . to separate achievement from intention, and it seems to me that a novel like *This Earth, My Brother* is a failure. It is

the kind of novel one would imagine gets written sometime, but I do not think it represents any permanent insight into the reality of African life.[19]

As we shall see, the novel is technically weak. But it is clearly the failure of the convention to provide the novel's meaning that demonstrates the decline of the convention.

Years after his return, Ammamu still finds the realities of Africa deeply unsettling. When the brother of his servant Yaro is beaten to death in a police station, Ammamu's wife Alice, for reasons never clarified, is herself deeply disturbed and flees to the coast. These developments suffice to tip the balance for Ammamu, who wanders wildly for three days, is found upon the beach in a mad torpor, and dies soon afterward. The cause of his death is never really made clear. Ammamu is absorbed by a jumble of memories of Europe and an awareness of present hard realities of life in Accra. But this issue is hardly sufficient to bring about his death. Professor Echeruo further compares Awoonor's novel to Armah's *The Beautyful Ones Are Not Yet Born*, quite correctly maintaining that the latter will endure whereas Awoonor's novel will be forgotten. For one cannot avoid the conclusion that *This Earth, My Brother* derives from Western and West African literatures considerably more than it does from life and the author's sensibility. The title vaguely suggests early Dylan Thomas.[20] Its pertinence to the novel is not clear other than to suggest the mortality of the protagonist, who does in fact die. But the connection is nonetheless very general indeed. For the hero's death is rather surprising. Nothing in the story suggests that he need be headed for disaster. Oblique references in the novel to Eliot's poem *The Waste Land*—"Fear death by water" (p. 39), "Fear death by guns" (p. 119), "Fear death by shit trucks" (p. 143)—support Echeruo's assertion that *This Earth, My Brother* becomes remote from African reality.

Similarly, Awoonor departs from the narrative text to interject Biblical or Bible-like passages, such as:

My strength is dried up like a potsherd; and my tongue cleaveth to my jaws; and thou has brought me into the dust of death. [P. 4]

And they smote him on the head with a reed and did spit upon him, and bowing their knees worshipped him. [St. Mark; p. 62]

Qui seminant in lacrimis, in gaudio metent. [P. 97]

New Treatments of the Been-to Convention

References of this nature are linked with quotations from Kierkegaard (pp. 145, 146, 187) and from Dante's *Inferno* (facing the title page; pp. 119, 185). Moreover, the narrative flow is frequently ruptured by lines like these:

> Memory dry as the legs of old women shall proclaim the shame of the crocodile as the shame of the alligator on the day of the lion.
> As man in the last throes of syphilis is screaming in a public latrine: It is coming!! [P. 147]

The context of the novel adds little meaning to these self-conscious, contrived passages.

Apparently, Awoonor has attempted a mosaic effect in the manner of *The Waste Land*, juxtaposing unlike elements without transition or explanation. The intent seems to be to reproduce Ammamu's consciousness.

Ammamu, the divided man, remembers not quite comprehensibly thus:

> The train swept through the greening countryside of England, once our mother country. We, the best of nature's freaks, African Intellectuals, are returning from Oxford where there still is a watering place by the name of a pub and we drowned our exile tears in gallons of good English beer. . . . Aren't we all dreaming of our native land in this great city once more on the breast of women in negligees, snoring in patriotic rhythm our national anthems and waving our miniature national flags at shit trucks roaring away in dark tropical evenings when moons are tired? Aren't we all, my brother? [P. 172]

But even with an understanding of the conflicting preoccupations of the been-to—painful memories of Europe, the shame-laden passion to be there once more, memories of nostalgia for Africa, and disgust with African reality—*This Earth, My Brother* fails as a novel. Its narrative line is too sketchy, almost lost in the incomprehensible, miniscule shards of the mosaic.

Even though Awoonor seems to have sufficient material for a successful novel, it is perhaps in part the very understanding of the fact that the repeated use of the been-to convention now calls for innovative treatment that causes the novel to fail. For *This Earth, My Brother* is indeed innovative, and the attempt is commendable. However, the composite of images, fragments of anecdotes, and literary references obtrudes rather than communicate enough of Ammamu's character and situation for us to understand him. We see him change, but we cannot tell why he does so. Finally, one suspects that Ammamu merely does what the convention says he is supposed to. This weakness of characterization reflects both a failure of technique and the fact that the convention has lost its original impact. Although Awoonor relies heavily on the convention to suggest the motives of his character, the convention has become too remote from African reality to clarify Ammamu's actions. So the story, often merely implied rather than presented, fails to achieve its intended effect.

The Edifice:
New Characterization for the Been-to

At a symposium of writers and scholars in Lagos in 1973, Kole Omotoso remarked that he was

> a member of a completely new generation. The gentlemen here [including writers Cyprian Ekwensi, J. P. Clark, Gabriel Okara, and John Updike] had only English and American literature before them when they were thinking of writing. When I started, I had their works to go on as well as sources of my own inspiration.[21]

Although he is a member of a new generation only in a figurative sense of the term, Omotoso, born in 1943, has come along late enough to have been shaped by the influence of the earlier writers and by a different set of historical circumstances. During his lifetime, Africa has seen the decline and end of colonialism and the rise of new nationalism. To Omotoso, the African encounter with the West is over; African nations are now engaged in self-development. The importation of Western elements is no longer of signal interest in and of itself. Rather, to Omotoso's view, that ongoing process is simply a thoroughly assimilated fact of the African present.[22] Although several important details seem to be missing from Omotoso's novel, this new perception of the been-to could be an important one, signaling a significant shift in West African sensibilities. Let us first consider the content and style of Omotoso's story and then turn to its possible implications.

New Treatments of the Been-to Convention

The matter-of-fact acceptance of Africa's present acquisition of the goods and sensibilities of the technological world is reflected in Omotoso's first work, *The Edifice*, published in 1971. In this work the theme of the been-to is presented in a significantly altered form. Dele, Omotoso's protagonist, ends considerably closer to the happily ambitious Brempong of Armah's *Fragments* than to Baako, that novel's thoughtful, troubled hero. The central problem of *The Edifice* is not that Dele finds himself an indigenous stranger. On the contrary, it is really his English wife, not he, who suffers the problems of cultural conflict. Her husband grows progressively estranged from her as he succeeds in the commerce and politics of the new Nigeria.

The novel begins in England, where the hero suffers the kind of discomforts that are conventionally treated in the been-to theme: loneliness, condescending racism, exploitative relationships. Although he supposedly has outgrown a childish desire to become white, he is very attracted to English women and has many affairs. Despite his conviction that he could never marry a white girl, he eventually meets Daisy, who changes his mind. Daisy, we are told (but not shown), reacts to him as to a full person. "She didn't think of me as some freak of nature, some trick upon the world."[23] She undertakes to study Yoruba, clear evidence that she is attracted to him as something considerably more substantive than a mere sexual exotic. Yet, when they marry, his misgivings begin to grow. "All through the marriage service I kept on remembering a funeral service I'd attended years ago. It was cold in the church. . . . There were few of my friends. . . . Those who came looked as if they were at a funeral service. My funeral" (p. 92).

Their subsequent life in Nigeria is presented from the point of view of Daisy, who bitterly recounts the tale of the disintegration of the marriage. Dele has changed dramatically. He engages in several affairs and even takes a second wife, another white woman. Daisy has been neglected by Dele and is not accepted by his family. Their son has died under mysterious circumstances while visiting Dele's parents. Daisy believes he has been murdered. Absolutely incapable of accepting any part of a polygamous marriage, she finally has the strength to break from her husband. As the novella ends, she wonders what she will do.

Although this story could have been material for a much longer novel, Omotoso has chosen to tell it in a very slight novella of fewer than twenty-five thousand words. The attempt is, on the whole, unsuccessful. While extremely interesting characterization is strongly suggested, the

several brief anecdotes that make up the novella do not permit development of the story's rich potential. Far too many questions are unan-
swered. Omotoso's fugitive characterization does not offer any understanding of the transition of Dele from the excellent young scholar who
loves English literature to the ruthless, self-centered young man on the
rise in the dangerous and demanding world of new nationalist politics.
We do see something of the character of Daisy, but too little is given for us
to understand the failure of the marriage. Of the woman who replaces
her, almost no information is given. Daisy knows very little about her
even though they share the same husband. Daisy says of her, "And how
could she consent to such an uncivilized thing as polygamy? But she was
an American, which explained many things" (p. 120).

This passage is characteristic of Omotoso's attempt to explain very
much with very little. The attempt produces many difficulties. Yet Omotoso did not intend to write a conventional novel. Asked if he considered
form and content well married in *The Edifice*, he responded:

> Yes. Remember, it was a process of deliberate imitation. It consists of
> mental action. It couldn't be a play. Most of it doesn't *happen*. This society
> doesn't have a tradition of reading, and not everything has to be explained
> to them anyway. They're familiar with these cases. Moreover, I get *bored*
> trying to develop a long analytical novel. All my novels are deliberately
> limited to about one hundred pages. So *The Edifice* is a deliberate intuitive,
> impressionistic kind of pastiche. [The Ibadan interview]

Although *The Edifice* may appeal to some Nigerian readers in part
because of its brevity, its style is far too feeble to support the complexities
of its themes. For *The Edifice* is full of implications. Omotoso's assertion
that the encounter with the West is over is contradicted by the drama of
his novella. The encounter has entered a different stage, perhaps, but it
remains an encounter indeed. Although the presence of the West is a
common fact in West Africa, it is still not an easy one. Therefore, we may
surmise that the been-to convention expresses a continuing truth about
West African life. Omotoso's words bear evidence to this contention.

> After all [he says], for Nigerians, going to Britain was a shattering expe-
> rience. When people come back, they describe the beauty, the wealth, the
> advance of the country, but not their suffering. So the novel is about the
> experience after the dreams have fallen away. The reasons why things
> happen are not made clear. But people's issues are private. People don't

like to talk about it. But Dele's behaviour is standardized. . . . The novel is also an expression of my disillusion with England. Yes, I almost packed in and came home; so, in order to reconcile the situation, I had to write the novel. [Ibid.]

Like many other been-to novels, then, *The Edifice* is in some ways autobiographical and, when it deals with student days in England, quite conventional. But this writer of the new generation has strong convictions about the conventional depiction of the newly returned been-to as

> blundering, undecided, confused personalities. They have lost grip of their traditional society and they are completely overwhelmed by the new society. In novel after play after poem, we have been so fed with this inept, unsure, blundering African that we are incapable of taking hold of the new way of life and bending it to our own use.[24]

This passage does not describe Dele. He represents a new kind of literary depiction of the been-to protagonist. He does not return impoverished. He is immediately successful at the university and later in politics. He is even able to reconcile conflicting attractions to Western and African values: in the African manner, he marries polygamously; the women he chooses are Westerners. That the first marriage fails is no sign of an indecisiveness on Dele's part, though it may reflect ineptitude and even worse failures. But Dele does not remain peripheral to his culture, judging it in the manner of Baako or Ammamu. On the contrary, he plunges into national life, aiming for a position of power when civil rule is returned to Nigeria. Although the characterization of *The Edifice* is so superficial that we know rather little of the adult Dele, one does not imagine that this ambitious young man would follow the example of earlier literary been-tos and dramatically resign his job on some matter of principle. Dele's values and motives are clear. At this point he is on a rising trajectory. That rise seems to be the highest good for him.

But whereas Dele's motives are clear, Omotoso's are not. The confusion and indecision that plague the protagonists of earlier been-to novels are based on moral conflict. The values that their foreign educations have given them are at odds with the way people act at home. The been-to heroes reject expediency, an act that exacts its price. Through these characters, their authors render unequivocable social criticism. Omotoso's been-to is at one with his society, even though Omotoso seems not to be. But Omotoso's shift from the point of view of Dele and from his presentation of him as a sympathetic character should have meaning. The difficulty is that too little is said. Omotoso claims that the second marriage indicates his own belief that (1) Nigeria simply cannot close out the world even if its initial contacts have been painful and (2) "one must go forward and be reconciled to what he has become." (the Ibadan interview)

These ideas are not apparent in the context of the novella, for what Dele has become is hardly admirable. One suspects that his political ascendancy will hardly benefit Nigeria. But perhaps there is more to the story than has been told. Perhaps Omotoso has conceived far more complex characters than he has presented, for *The Edifice* suggests complexity without actually engaging it. In any case, *The Edifice* indicates a new stage for the been-to convention, even though the novel merely points to intricately interwoven issues. The been-to protagonist in this work has been given a new form that suggests that the frequent repetition of the convention and changing West African conditions are both affecting the literature of the region.

Why Are We So Blest?
The Ritual Death of the Been-to

In the next novel we are to consider, Armah's third work, *Why Are We So Blest?* two conventionally divided, paralyzed been-tos are the central figures. In this work published in 1972, the been-tos display much the same old longings and uncertainties. Yet the been-to is given a new role, a new characterization that can be seen as the completion of a psychological process. The been-to is no mythic hero in this work. He brings back no fire, no golden fleece for his people or himself. He does not extend the scope of their consciousness. On the contrary, Armah castigates the been-to in the most outspoken terms of any West African novel. The Western scar marks a fatal wound, Armah tells us. The conventional university training in the West is far worse than a merely difficult experience for the young elite. The protagonists of *Why Are We So Blest?* uncompromisingly, unrelentingly assert and demonstrate that it is a psychically fatal undertaking. Further, Armah maintains that the been-to is a poor dupe who has been carefully selected by undefined, destructive Western powers. His potential for Africa's good has been subtly fashioned into an instrument of its continued economic and cultural destruction.

Admittedly, Armah's committed position lends the novel no little power. His considerable talents are generally apparent throughout. Despite the merit to Armah's new conception of the been-to, his almost undeviating preoccupation with this thesis robs *Why Are We So Blest?* of much of its potential as art and, thereby, much of its political power as well. Nevertheless, the novel occupies a singular position in West African literary history. It signals a process undergone because it represents a signal psychological break from the West.

Considering Armah's uses of the fictive devices of narrative frame, setting and characterization in particular, we shall be able to assess these two central properties of the work, its importance in the history of West African fiction, and its weakness as art for being a thesis-ridden work.

Why Are We So Blest? is short, approximately eighty-five thousand words in length. It purports to consist in part of the journals of the principal figures, Modin Dofu and Aimée Reitsch. The third principal character, Solo Nkonam, appears as a kind of editor of their writings. Their words come to the reader supposedly through his selection and somewhat after the action they describe has occurred. This latter characteristic imparts something of a static quality to the events, as if they were material for analysis. Solo's own comments on the words of the other two place things at a further remove, which separation, however, permits his reflections upon the significance of events.

Excerpts from Aimée's journal compose the most limited commentary of the three. There are only six entries for her, a total of twenty-four pages. Modin is given thirteen excerpts, for a total of ninety-eight pages. His is the principal voice. Solo is given eighty-three pages in a total of ten entries. There is a suggestion that his is possibly Armah's voice. On page 71 an entry entitled "Solo" reads:

> The entries in the African's book do not all bear dates. The things he wrote of were in general not events; they were more like concatenations of ideas. Some I have not understood at all. The greater part have a meaning outside the final line of his life, being like tentative excursions away from the main route. I have left them alone.
>
> The Book of the American girl does not contain much that promises to be understandable. A portion is open to the understanding mind in a pointless kind of way: it may be understood, but its understanding does not add or subtract anything from the grasping faculty. Chance encounters, notes from a variety of sources which might as well, with a small number of exceptions, remain incoherent—the tissue of an aimless existence.
>
> I do not in the end understand his attraction to her. The truth is, I do

not want to understand. I am afraid to understand. Afraid, ultimately, for myself.[25]

This passage establishes Solo as an authorial or, at least, an editorial agency. Hereafter, the selections that appear in Aimée's, Modin's, or his own words are purportedly the result of Solo's selection. His own characterization is present in his words, so he functions both as participant and as shaping force of the work. Armah thus solves the difficulties of the shifting points of view. The total work has the quality of being shaped by one person who effects the shifts when the narrative line provides an appropriate point of departure. The various selections from the journals produce a distorted chronological order, but the final result ultimately includes the beginning, middle, and end of a complete story.

Armah's method places the events in a context of hopelessness, a prevailing mood of the novel. The first words, Solo's, read:

> Even before my death I have become a ghost, wandering about the face of the earth, moving with a freedom I have not chosen, something whose unsettling abundance I am impotent to use. There is no contact possible. Life goes on around me, and with a clarity that has grown sharply painful, I see it flow like a stream in slow motion. . . . Only there is no portion of the stream . . . into which I can fling myself and say: "Here I belong. This is my home." [P. 11]

The first example of Modin's entries a dozen pages or so later begins on a similarly despairing note.

> The directions made available to me within this arrangement are all suicidal. I am supposed to get myself destroyed out of my own free-seeming choice. Earl is a suicide. All these integrants with their white wives are suicides. How to avoid their death? All other paths seem closed. [P. 31]

Solo is a been-to who considers himself useless in Africa. His experiences in Portugal have undermined him. A would-be writer, he cannot produce. Modin is still in the United States at the point of his first entry in the book. He has understood that America is producing a monster in him. He has stopped attending lectures at Harvard. He is convinced that "all existent methods are absurd and deadly outside of a revolutionary commitment to Africa" (ibid.), but as yet he is unable to act upon that understanding.

Although Aimée's first entry is considerably more opaque regarding her character, the thematic intent of the passage is pellucid. It purports to be a transcript of a taped secret visit she has made to an African woman who reports to her how the whites have captured a great revolutionary leader and imprisoned him, whereupon "they turned him into a child" (p. 41). Thus Aimée's first entry associates her with the destructive forces of the white race.

With the introduction of each of his central characters, then, Armah has presented the theme of the destructiveness of the white race and its malevolent intent in Africa. Throughout the novel the theme is reiterated. Solo, destroyed by his Western experience, constantly bemoans his fate without even being able to effect any action that will lead to a change in his condition. Modin tries very diligently, up to a certain point, to bring off a self-redeeming act, participating in the revolution in Africa. But the revolutionaries have a clear understanding of the truth of something he has deeply feared, that his Western education has already proven to be a fatal poison. They reject him, and he eventually dies a pointless death. Aimée, despite herself, finally becomes the very embodiment of the destructive Western forces.

Armah sets forth his theme in each of the notebooks of his characters. The implicit logic of development is that Solo, a blocked writer, afflicted by the paralysis of the been-to, sees the world through the limiting perspective of his condition. What he shows of Aimée's and Modin's journals is selected to explain Modin's case and his own.

One of the novel's major weaknesses is that the selection excludes almost all details of the texture of life. The setting is never more than one stage or another arranged as a backdrop to Armah's theme. Action takes place in the United States at Harvard and briefly in Washington, D.C., in Portugal, and in fictional regions of Africa. Armah devotes scant attention to the physical details of his Western settings, limiting himself to citing place names: Washington, D.C., New York, Harvard, Lisbon. There are almost no descriptions of place. Armah's technique of the journal format renders the omissions perfectly plausible, but the novel suffers from a sense of disembodiment nonetheless.

The fictional African settings are treated with somewhat more detail. On page 15, Solo notes, "Laccryville is a hilly city, and the area in which I live is one of the hilliest." The next specific details come thirty-three pages farther on.

Halfway down the road from the Post Office to the main harbor gate is the Bureau. It occupies two spacious floors of a large building at the intersection of the wide central avenue and the harbor road. All the roads and streets are being renamed. . . . It is being reported that the one on which the Bureau stands may be named after Fanon. The Bureau would then have on paper a fitting address for a center of revolutionary activity:

Bureau of the Peoples Union of Congheria
1, rue Frantz Fanon

What goes on inside the Bureau itself, however, will always be a different matter. [P. 48]

This passage is indicative of Armah's method. The physical setting in this novel is considerably less significant than his idea. Setting merely serves as a basis for the introduction of a theme, in this case, that of the failures of revolutions. Laccryville, the capital of Afrasia, has completed its revolution against the French at the cost of one million lives. In the hospital, Solo meets an Afrasian veteran who has lost a leg. The man passes the time of his convalescence reading about the French revolution. Who won, he wants to know. His question is not really about French history, but about his own country's war, for there are no signs of victory. The same old forces seem to be in power. Solo expects the same conditions to prevail in the revolt of his own country, Congheria, against the Portuguese. A series of photographs in the revolutionary headquarters is ominously suggestive.

The first shots are historical. In them everything seems exaggeratedly rudimentary. The soldiers of the rebellion appear to be a confused crowd, wearing assorted clothes. Then there is a rapid progression through stages in which only a few are in uniform, then most, until in the last pictures everyone is in uniform. Not only that. Now there are different types of uniform for different rank, the colors getting lighter with increasing rank. Dominating all the pictures is a huge portrait of the leader of the UPC, looking sternly down upon his followers through his spectacles. Under the picture is the caption:

Ignace Sendoulwa
Premier Militant

The man is shown wearing an immaculate white suit. [P. 49]

Once again setting functions to demonstrate theme, in this instance quite legitimately. The most detailed description of the setting is given in the final pages of the novel wherein Modin's death, the embodiment of the central theme, is enacted. In this portion of the novel one feels that the plot has been forced into an unlikely development in order to produce an appropriate setting for the action. The country seems still to be Afrasia, but the reader cannot be certain. Modin and Aimée are on the southern, or perhaps northern, edge of the Sahara desert, which they are attempting to cross as a kind of ill-conceived "revolutionary" exploit. Modin's journal describes the scene.

> Ousnia. Small town, small houses. The new ones are whitewashed. The old ones are more numerous, smaller, the color of the sand all around, maybe a shade deeper. Outside the town the only change is from rock to sand, sand to rock.
>
> Ousnia is in a hollow. The cold here is the worst it has been so far. It gets worse everyday. The road is bluish from its new tar. It dips down into the hollow then rises straight on the southern side. [P. 277]

As they travel deeper into the desert, Armah uses the setting to evoke notions of dread. The light is "a blade-blue color" and turns into "sharp stinging shafts of coldness visible without giving off any heat" (ibid.). Modin and Aimée are told that the road leads to a petroleum drilling installation, then a hundred kilometers farther, to a French military base, neither of which is on the map.

Their being in unmapped territory heightens the sense of the danger and folly of the black man and the white woman, hitchhiking into the barren desert where the racist colonial French troops still enjoy absolute control. The setting continues to support Armah's theme. Modin writes further: "This place is amazing. There is nothing here, not even sand. Everything is hard, stony" (p. 278). The final scene, Modin's murder, is set in sand dunes, where no specific traits distinguish one spot from another.

Perhaps Armah would have done well to have avoided the ambiguity and confusion of his fictional African settings. One is not certain if the action occurs in North Africa or West Africa. Some descriptions suggest that Afrasia is the fictional counterpart of Algeria, but the characters are black, sub-Saharan Africans. One cannot be certain whether Aimée and Modin move north or south as they travel into the desert. Clarifying these details, however, is obviously not Armah's concern. He wishes to oppose a stereotypic idea of Africa against stereotypic ideas of the West.

So contradictions and uncertainties in his settings do not deter him. Setting only serves to provide places where action and theme can merge.

But once again Armah's preoccupation with his theme undermines the novel's potential for conviction. The Africa of *Why Are We So Blest?* is a mere oversimplified stage-set Africa, an Africa bereft of the realities of its manifold contradictions.

Armah's excessive concern with thesis similarly restricts the development of his characters. Solo is merely the paralyzed been-to. He frequently restates his ineffectualness. In fact, if the novel is seen as his statement in which he uses selections from the journals of Modin and Aimée to make his points, its whole purpose seems to be to demonstrate his ruin. The subject of his paralysis dominates his statement. He offers no hope, demonstrates no struggle for revitalization. Finally we are exasperated with him. Why doesn't the man move? A rejected proposal of marriage does not warrant such a prolonged total depression. Armah is capable of much more complex characterization as the character of Sylvia shows. But the theme of *Why Are We So Blest?* requires such a ruined spokesman. Modin is, finally, merely the victim of the savage appetites of white men and white women. Aimée, despite her love for Modin, is his destroyer. The minor characters compose a parade of thinly developed stereotypes. Professor Earl Lynch is the poor, duped Afro-American intellectual who has no understanding of the concessions he has made for his position at Harvard. Naita is the American black woman, half mother, half mistress, whose affection for Modin is masked by stern admonitions. Mr. Oppenhardt is the embodiment of the mysterious Malevolent Western Power. He funds Modin's Western education but will accept no disagreement from him. Professor Henry Jefferson is a Harvard Africanist whose professional discipline Armah never makes clear. He introduces Modin to Mrs. Jefferson, who then plays a role of The Unsatisfied Wife, craving Modin's Mysterious Dark Sexuality. Jefferson reveals his conventional hypocrisy when he stabs Modin, almost fatally, upon hearing Mrs. Jefferson's orgasmic moans filling the summer night. That it is as "Mrs. Jefferson" that Modin thinks of her demonstrates the narrowness of her role as the wife of a professor. Only once does Modin refer to her as "Sandra." But even then, the context is one that confines her within a stereotypic role that supports the novel's overriding thesis.

This is youth searching for the excitement of life lived at the level of culture's basic myths. My new friend is the Western European damsel in distress, the valued prize after the conflict between the dragon and knight. But the conflict now grows in complexity. There is no knowing who the knight may be and who the dragon, for this is one of history's crossroads, and old values may or may not get changed. Standing at the crossroads, Sandra, the American youth, prize after the great cataclysm, from which she would be the only certain gainer. [P. 157]

Modin's shallow perception of Sandra Jefferson seems to be indistinguishable from that of the author. Armah does not develop the complexities of their relationship. Modin seems to be either merely exploitative, without concern for the well-being of the people who have befriended him, or strangely passive, simply obedient to the passionate pleas of Mrs. Jefferson. Contrivance is apparent, for as Modin's journal entry makes clear, Mrs. Jefferson is essentially the representative of an aspect of the relationship between Africa and the West.

Perhaps the most successfully realized character of the novel is Sylvia, Solo's white fiancée in Lisbon, who proves too weak to marry an African. Within the limits of six pages, Armah, with remarkable selection, develops the characterization of a kind and compassionate young woman. Her romantic and idealistic affair with Solo ends when her Portuguese friends lead her to confront some truths about herself she has not known before. The strength of this characterization derives from Armah's willingness to withhold analysis and, for the most part, to let the events speak for themselves. The characterization of the major figures, Aimée, Modin, and Solo, is closely linked with the novel's central intent of presenting specific discursive ideas. Modin's journal sets forth the principal position to which the work is bound.

What a farce, scholarships! That blood money never went to any of us for our intelligence. It was always payment for obedience. BEFORE THE WHITE MAN CAME. Ten pages of blood and savagery. THE WHITE MAN COMES. ENLIGHTENMENT, CIVILIZATION, PROGRESS, DEVELOPMENT—any of the white man's words for the white man's rule. It takes obedience, not intelligence to accept that as knowledge.

Factors then, scholarship holders, B.A.s, M.A.s, Ph.D.s now, the privileged servants of white empire, factors then, factors now. The physical walls stand unused now. The curious can go and look at them, as if slavery belonged to a past history. The destruction has reached higher, that is all. The factors' pay is now given in advance, and sold men are not mentioned, not seen in any mind. Their price is given the factor for some mythical quality of his dead spirit. His murdered intelligence is praised. The easier for the givers of these scholarships, this factors' pay, to *structure* the recipients' lives into modern factorship.

A standard of living above the African level. Why must the African level be kept so low—and who is being trained to keep it low? Standards of living maintained by structures erected against fellow Africans. That talk of intelligence and desert is the wall to hide us from those we're selling.

Naita is right. The educated Africans, the Westernized African successes are contemptible worms.

"Exceptionally uncreative people," she said.

Happy to get the degrees, then go home and relax on the shoulders of our sold people. The end of a Western education is not work but self-indulgence. An education for worms and slugs. [Pp. 160–161]

A characteristically powerful authorial assertion by Armah, this one is radically at odds with the positions expressed in his first two novels and in other been-to novels as well. Here his sympathies are clearly with African peoples, his enmity directed toward the West. In *Fragments* and *The Beautyful Ones Are Not Yet Born*, whereas the West is castigated as something of a destructive force for Africa, Armah specifically attacks the Ghanaians for consistently selecting the worst that Western civilization has to offer. In both novels, there is a strong implication that certain Western moral principles and those of traditional Ghana are vastly superior to the moral chaos of Ghana of the 1960s. True, Modin and Solo are presented as morally ineffectual and the revolutionaries are shown to be corrupted by their very success. These cases demonstrate African inadequacies. But at the same time, as we have seen, the real target is the West, where both men and women, driven by various appetites, would consume the African vitality.

To meet this goal, Armah has very clearly streamlined Aimée's characterization within a single figure. She is initially given two dominant motivations, perhaps not disconnected, African freedom and sexual fulfillment. Her first entry in the novel is an account of her visit to a famous African woman revolutionary. Even though Mzee Nyambura speaks to her of revolutionary activities (in a very guarded manner), the journal entry demonstrates Aimée's sympathies with African revolutions. We are invited by Armah's implication to be sympathetic to Aimée. But almost nothing of her character emerges in this short passage.

Subsequently, her meeting with Modin is hardly credible, but Armah does succeed in presenting her in an ominous light. Modin's journal reads, "When I need more money I sign on as a subject for experimenting graduate students, mainly in the Psycho Lab. That was where I met Aimée (p. 168)." The juxtaposition of *Aimée* and *Psycho* is not accidental. Out of a need for sensation she is serving as a subject for experiments that measure the subject's level of tolerance of pain inflicted in the form of electric shock. Several people are present, participants and technicians.

> "Hey, do we get to choose where?" [she asks.]
> "Where what?" . . .
> "Where we get shocked."
> "Why, do you have any special preference?"
> "My clit," Aimée said.
> "Your who?" There had been a kind of inviting playfulness in Aimée's voice, an indication that what she said did not have to be taken too seriously. Joel's question disregarded this entirely.
> "My cllitt-torr-riss."
> Joel's face turned whiter. . . . "We don't give far-out orgasms here. Sorry."
> "Don't apologize. I wouldn't get one anyway." The playfulness had vanished from her tone. [P. 171–172]

This scene, necessary for her characterization, demonstrates its flaws. Her acknowledgement of her frigidity is obviously too public an act. Far more effective might have been an entry from her journal reporting a more private attempt. Such a dialogue among strangers in a crowded room is very unlikely. Again, the novel's theme accounts for its presence. Aimée's role is to act as a perverted Western appetite that requires destructive means for satisfaction.

Failing to achieve an orgasm by clinical means, Aimée is finally able to succeed by persuading Modin to participate in a debasing fantasy. As they copulate, they pretend that he is Mwangi, a houseboy, and she is his colonial mistress.

> "Don't stop! [she cries] I found the scene. Help me."
> "What scene?" I asked.
> "Kansa. The rebellion, my period. My husband is coming home. He's a settler. I don't know when. It's dangerous. You're the boy."
> "And Mwangi is my name."
> "Yes, yes, yes, yes dooon't stop! Yes!" [P. 199]

Although Modin refuses to play the part in this scene, he later consents, fully understanding the destructiveness of their relationship. For Aimée finally becomes only destructive. It is her spoiled willfulness that leads to Modin's death. Even though Aimée has some uncertain revolutionary impulses, it is readily apparent that this interest is merely another sign of her hunger for sensation.

Sexual hunger and romantic ideas of political realities in Africa could well be believable traits of a sympathetic character. But Armah's depiction of Aimée fails in that he shows these traits to excess and gives her almost no others. As is true of other aspects of the novel, Aimée's characterization is all too obviously purposive. She cannot engage our sympathies, for the theme requires a villainess.

Modin's own case illustrates the point he makes in his journal. Determined that he will not become a modern-day factor, the African entrepreneur of slaves, Modin returns to Africa to join the revolutionaries. But he takes Aimée with him. The obvious contradictions of these acts would perhaps be believable in one who is less aware than Modin. But Armah has made him both conscious of and articulate about the plight of the African in the West. One wonders whether one who writes, "That man, a black man irretrievably caught in total whiteness, is humanity at its most destroyed" (p. 163), would undertake enterprise so laden with contradictions. Certainly the point is clear. Modin's folly is caused by the disease he complains of throughout.

Yet if some of his acts are merely doubtful, the final scenes are past all credibility. The pointless hitchhiking scene into the Sahara occupied by racist French troops might be possible, but not the following. Modin is tied naked to the back of a jeep. The soldiers carry the naked Aimée to him. "They held me, legs apart, and rubbed up and down against Modin. They succeeded in arousing him. He stared in my direction but not at me. When his prick got hard they slid my body forward so he entered me, then they snatched me back at once" (p. 286). One of the soldiers tries to shoot Modin's erect penis. When he misses, the men slip a wire noose around the organ. Even under these trying circumstances Modin's sexuality is resilient.

They used me to get Modin hard. The wounded man gave a yell of pain and pulled hard on the wire. . . . The snapping off of the tip of Modin's prick was slow. I thought it would fall just like that, but the wire cut into his flesh and then in spite of all that tension nothing seemed to happen. Modin did not scream. I was thinking the wire had broken when the tip of his penis snapped off and hung by just a bit of skin from the bottom.

. . . .

Modin started bleeding. The blood curved out in a little stream that jerked outward about every second. I reached him and without thinking what I was doing I kissed him. His blood filled my mouth. I swallowed it. I wanted him to speak to me. . . .

I asked him "Do you love me?" [P. 287–288]

The horror of the scene urges one to dismiss it in some way. It is further undermined by the grisly comedy of its physical impossibilities and the ludicrousness of Aimée's question. Excess and contrivance are everywhere apparent. Armah has struggled to bring us to this symbolic image of the black man crucified on the back of a jeep as his mutilated penis pumps blood into the mouth of a white woman. But the inexplicable desert trip and the sudden arrival of the murderous French soldiers are nonetheless gratuitous. It is perfectly apparent that the thesis that has shaped the novel throughout is simply being given a final illustration.

Even though *Why Are We So Blest?* is a seriously flawed work, it makes a significant change in the development of the been-to convention. The nature of the been-to image and the frequency of its expression reflect a collective attitude of African elites who have undergone the experience of something comparable. The diminishing use of the image and its loss of effectiveness are different indications of changes in West African sensibilities. Earlier been-to novels reflected ambiguous attitudes toward the West. This novel conveys no lingering ambiguities.

The West is a powerful attraction, but it is solely a destructive force; Africa must free itself of its passion for the West—this is Armah's message. We are not invited to sympathize with the romantic conflicts of the divided man. The unremitting call of the novel is for the disengagement of Africa from Western involvement. It is unfortunate that this major assertion of the need for cultural independence is not embodied in a novel more genuinely reflective of Armah's significant talents.

Although *Why Are We So Blest?* is seriously weakened by Armah's lack of objectivity, the emotional intensity of the novel attests to the continuing significance of the theme. Modin's ritual death represents a statement of dual protest against the destructive West and the victimized Africa. The acts of the final scenes of the novel are as ceremonial as rites performed upon an altar. The soldiers swoop into view out of the formless desert. Their arrival is surprising but somehow as inevitable as that of Cocteau's mysterious motorcyclists. Aimée, a kind of priestess of Western malevolence, in their last embrace draws Modin's lifeblood. Modin does not speak or cry out. His self-destructive passion for Aimée has finally led him to total passivity. Both victim and killers are the object of Armah's attack. Even though the character has been altered and given a new value, even ritually sacrificed, Modin is yet another rendering of the archetypal figure.

Thus, although the convention has undergone a period of eclipse, it very likely will continue to appear in West African fiction. For as Carl Jung has asserted, "The archetype is a tendency to form representations of a motif—representations that can vary a great deal in detail without losing their basic pattern . . . they are, indeed, an instinctive trend, as marked as the impulse of birds to build nests or ants to form organized colonies."[26]

Chapter Five

Conclusion

The progress of the been-to convention in West African fiction seems to lend itself to depiction in terms of an image of an arching rise followed by an apparent decline. However, evidence suggests that the convention is deeply significant and its continuing recurrent use is likely. We have seen how the convention appeared in the first West African novel, Casely-Hayford's *Ethiopia Unbound,* and how it retained an important place in African literature for more than fifty years before it began to fade from significance. Further, we have seen that the most accomplished of the novels employing the convention, while reflective of significant social realities, have another, more universal import, the mythic theme of metamorphosis. In this final chapter, I wish to complete my account of the history of the convention. I shall present (1) a brief summary of the major changes that the convention has undergone, (2) some verification of my assertions regarding the convention, based on recent developments in Africa, and (3) an assessment of the significance of the been-to convention in African literature and in world literature.

First, we need a general summary of what we have seen. Since the convention is an account of the deepest meanings of social and spiritual metamorphosis, it is supremely logical that the form itself has undergone a similar kind of fundamental change. Indeed, the pattern of change is readily traceable: Kwamankra, the first been-to hero in Casely-Hayford's *Ethiopia Unbound,* is seen as threatening and dangerous as he introduces the radical notions of Ethiopianism to his countrymen under the eyes of their colonial masters. Camara Laye's dark child is determinedly sent abroad by his loving parents. Though they weep at his departure, overcome by the historical force that sweeps their child from them, they are powerless to prevent his going. But when Samba Diallo's family, a little later, sends him to France, it does so with misgivings. With far greater understanding than the dark child's parents, Diallo's people know they have taken a gamble. They are later to learn that the odds are overwhelmingly against them. An Islamic mystical oneness with the Divine Being is incompatible with the "Western exile of the soul."[1] Although Obi Okonkwo sees his University of London degree as the philosopher's stone, his case bears witness to the high cost its powers of transformation can exact. Baako's even deeper understanding of Africa's course of development extends the limits of the issue of transformation. Armah demonstrates that the social change is accompanied by a deep spiritual transformation of the most threatening kind. Still later, Kole Omotoso's hero Dele of *The Edifice* extends the presentation of Africa's historical change in yet another way. Dele is not outside his culture, judging his country's excesses. On the contrary, he has joined that corrupt society and struggles on its terms for political leadership. Modin is Armah's image of Africa's new crop; the Most Royal Lady of *Ambiguous Adventure* hoped that the new crop of the next generation would blossom from the soil of its European education as a vigorous new form of African life. Armah presents Modin as a poisoned new growth that threatens the life of all of Africa.

During its course, the convention has presented the been-to protagonist first as a rather conventional hero, then as a mythic hero. Later, in Omotoso's version, the been-to is given genuinely sinister characteristics. Finally, in *Why Are We So Blest?* Armah presents the been-to as a kind of combination victim and archvillain.

As we shall see next, the continued life of the convention seems to be verified by the continuing change in the role of the been-to protagonist. Continuing developments in African fiction and in African social reality tend to confirm the major assessments of this study. Let us first consider two novels published in the midseventies which are further evidence that the been-to convention has yet to run its course.

In 1967, Wole Soyinka complained that the African writer was guilty of

fabricating a magnitude of unfelt abstractions. Insolated by his very position in society, he mistook his own personal and temporary cultural predicament for the predicament of his entire society and turned attention from what was really happening to that society. He even tried to give society something that the society had never lost—its identity.[2]

This opinion was quite at odds with the theme of *The Interpreters*, which Soyinka had published two years before; the young been-tos in that novel serve as judges of Nigerian morality. But, as we have seen, other novels in the convention itself bear evidence to support his remarks. Ammamu of *This Earth, My Brother*, Baako of *Fragments*, and Obi of *No Longer at Ease*, for example, are quite isolated from their societies. Yet, at the same time, the novelists suggest that the protagonist is a kind of special representative of his society.

Is the convention truly, as Soyinka implies, merely an indulgence of the elite, which has become incapable of distinguishing personal or class problems from those of the entire culture? The issue is more complex Soyinka suggests, for, while his commentary is directed against the been-to convention, the hero of his novel *Season of Anomy* (1974), is a been-to. The hero, Ofeyi, is not a divided man, however. He does not suffer any confusion of identity. His Western education has not caused him any deep trauma. Yet, like other been-to protagonists before him, Ofeyi protests the corruption of his professional superiors. Like Baako and Sekoni, he defiantly resigns his position. The response of one company official is significant. He "wondered why such a fuss should be made over a gesture that was predictable of such stereotypes as Ofeyi."[3]

Terms that suggest Soyinka's fatigue with the convention, "predictable," "typical," and "stereotype," mark his passage. Yet Ofeyi *is* in fact a been-to and the conventional scene *does* occur.

But *Season of Anomy* is not a been-to novel in the standard sense of the earlier uses of the convention. The novel's subject reflects the growing interest of West African writers in internal African issues.[4] *Season of Anomy* is concerned almost wholly with an analogue of the Nigerian civil war. Although there is some reference to the political dominance of Western powers, the real issue is the matter of the Nigerian civil warfare. Ofeyi's foreign education is of no particular importance. It is included seemingly as something that someone of Ofeyi's talents and social class might be expected, as a matter of course, to have undergone. Why then is any point made of the fact? Perhaps it is that even though one meaning of the drama of the been-to convention has been played out, other factors of African cultural reality continue to require that the novel's hero be a been-to.

Another indication of the changing nature of West African fiction is Ayi Kwei Armah's *Two Thousand Seasons* (1973), published, quite significantly, in the East African Publishing House of Nairobi and not, as yet, in the West. The cover of the book notes that Armah has lived in Dar es Salaam since 1970. He has removed himself not only from the United States, where he had studied and taught for several years, but from West Africa as well. The novel chronicles a long campaign against Africans by Westerners. It ends on a cautiously hopeful note.

> Discouraging is loss, discouraging even the mere contemplation of the destroyers' massive weapons of death. But we have seen the destroyers' force hurled against us turn to strength against the hurlers, and we know our way lies beyond despair: far beyond despair our way, the way.[5]

Armah's new focus seems to grow logically out of the focus of his third novel. Although no been-to appears in the novel, it is clear that Armah has taken on the issue of Africa and the West in far broader terms.

Another verification of the fact that the convention still lives lies in this statement: even though been-tos compose a miniscule portion of West African society, the convention treats a deeply felt issue. That assertion is strongly supported by this article from the *New York Times* of December 1974:

> Africans who for reasons of choice or exile have spent long periods in Europe or America often experienced strains on returning home. Some, such as Malawi's president Kamuzu Banda, who spent so many years abroad that he could speak the native chiNyanja only falteringly on his return home in 1958, have had visible difficulty reconciling their Western habits with their African tradition. So too have some Tanzanian students who return from the fleshpots of Western universities to the austerity of a socialist country bent on eliminating privilege. In Somalia or Uganda, fashion-conscious young men and women may return to find tight trousers and miniskirts forbidden by law.[6]

As this present study has demonstrated, the cultural shock that the been-to undergoes derives from matters considerably more basic than fashion edicts. The report of conditions in Chad, moreover, reveals an emotional milieu very similar to that depicted in many been-to novels. The reporter tells us that in Chad there is the very lively possibility of encountering

> a new kind of culture shock, that felt by the small number of Africans who weather the rigors of Western education in Europe or America and return home not to positions of honor and respect, but to a series of humiliations.
> Only in one country, Chad, is this meant to happen. There, the educated urbanized elite is being forced to take part in a tribal initiation rite called Yondo. Teachers, clergymen, bankers and businessmen are among those who are, it is reported, hauled off for six weeks or more into the bush, where they undergo beatings, burnings, scarrings and other trials, supposedly to purge them of their Western ways. Refusal to take part may mean death, probably a nasty one.[7]

The report seems to lend considerable authority to *Why Are We So Blest?* It appears that Armah would find vigorous supporters in Chad for his novel's statement regarding the been-to. The affinity between the ritual of Yondo and *Why Are We So Blest?* is quite suggestive. It brings us back to Soyinka's complaint against African literature. The been-to convention might well be called "Yondo literature" but for the fact that the use of the literary convention is generally not so reactionary. The author's aim, in most cases, has been understanding and accommodation. But, as Soyinka notes, the novels of the convention have been produced by members of the elite. On the other hand, Yondo is an act of the common people. The act suggests that they are beginning to feel the disturbing tremors of cultural change and to respond in their turn with a protective ritual.

In a study that aids our understanding of the apparent contradiction in the rise of Yondo and the decline of the convention, Lillian Feder tells of an essential relationship between ritual practices and myth in ancient societies. Myth, she says, "clarified the prescribed action of the rites, and the rites enacted mythical narrative in stylized dramatic form."[8] In this case, we can assume that the mythic novels of the convention and the Yondo ritual are quite independent of each other, differing responses to the same cultural reality. Yet the practice of Yondo seems to call Soyinka's complaint into question. Seemingly, the fears that the members of the elite have experienced are becoming widespread. So we must conclude that, in fact, the decline of the convention and the newly instigated practice of Yondo are not really contradictions. In fact, the practice of Yondo verifies the psychological truths underlying the convention.

Then what are we to make of Ofeyi of *Season of Anomy*? Such a character is simply reflective of cultural reality. His identity is Nigerian, his outlook worldly but concerned with his nation. For him, to be a been-to is a simple fact. It carries no mythic import. Nonetheless, to resolve the seeming contradictions, we must conclude that for many West Africans a change of mythic import has occurred, some significant degree of Westernization.

Ofeyi's unquestioning sense of his identity indicates that change. There is no conflict for him for on his social level the been-to has become a common phenomenon. He is no indigenous stranger, for now there are thousands like him. The history of been-to conventions suggests that the privileged class has undertaken the process first and, despite its costs, seems to have survived it. Now we can expect the rest of society to encounter the process on its own terms. The Chadian ritual of Yondo suggests that at this next stage of the cultural interchange, traditional African elements will be particularly assertive. More significantly for our purposes, the ritual demonstrates the depth of feeling associated with the issue of the been-to, particularly a need to confront the mysteries of metamorphosis.

Finally, it must be said that even though our study has remained focused upon the been-to convention as an aspect of West African fiction, its significance is universal. African literature, in general, is itself very much like a been-to. Having traveled into the world at large, it is likely to be forever affected. Bernth Lindfors, a scholar and critic of African fiction, correctly warns his colleagues.

> [There] are sensitive zones—the inner sanctuaries and sacred groves which are accessible only to those within a society who have grown up learning [its] passwords . . . [consequently] foreign critics . . . should not attempt to brazenly trespass on territory that belongs to others who acquired the indigenous grammar while young and thus know how to decode and interpret the deep structures underlying their own semantic universe.[9]

Although Lindfors's words must be considered, it is also true that African literature is now becoming a force influencing Western culture. *Our* perception, *our* understanding, the deep grammar of *our* sensibilities will perhaps be shaped by it, just as they have been profoundly touched and altered by the precision and power of West African sculpture, which, since the early part of this century, has fundamentally affected Western perception. Consequently, there are more sacred groves than one to be considered. This is particularly true of the convention of the been-to. For even though this body of West African novels contains uneven artistic achievements, even some rather poor novels, it contains some notable works as well. Moreover, all the works in the convention strongly indicate the validity of Jacques Maquet's incisive comment regarding one aspect of the relationship between Africa and the West.

> The isolation of modern Western man seems to increase as the population of his cities grow[s] and his communications intensify; man's insecurity seems to grow greater as his mastery of the world becomes surer. The African has learned wonderfully to make the best of his situation by developing to the utmost the possibilities of harmony and adaptation inherent in the social nature of man.[10]

We have seen that the authors' most careful attention in these novels is often directed to these issues of social harmony and adaptation and, above all, human possibility. In that preoccupation, these African authors present us another seeming contradiction, the most instructive of all. Not only is the been-to convention an account of Africa's opening up to the West. It may also be seen, as the works employing the convention are more widely read, to represent one stage in the measured opening up of the West to the cultural influences of Africa.

Whether African writers will produce other been-to novels is uncertain. There is every indication that they will. Certainly, the major works of the convention, such as *Fragments*, *No Longer at Ease*, *The Radiance of the King*, and *Ambiguous Adventure*, are deeply engaging, well-wrought novels, the reputations and significance of which will endure. And the frequently retold tale of the been-to, despite the changing patterns of the convention, will retain a power to move us because, while it is concerned with a very specific aspect of African history, it also deals with one of the most basic givens of human experience—mutability.

Notes

CHAPTER ONE

1. Charles R. Larson, *The Emergence of African Fiction* (Bloomington: Indiana University Press, 1971), pp. 3–4.
2. Hans Zell and Helene Silver, *A Reader's Guide to African Literature* (New York: Africana Publishing Corp., 1971), p. ix.
3. Although the term *been-to* may originally have been purely descriptive or even honorific, it is now used pejoratively. The satirical implication is that one who frequently refers to his trip to Europe or America is suggesting that his was a long stay of study and personal development, during which he acquired genuine education and new tastes. In fact, however, such persons often have merely *been to* England or France or wherever, merely touching down, as it were, and then returning with a cluster of affectations. Augustan England had its counterpart been-to who frequently let fall details of his voyage to Italy, however brief it may actually have been. In this study, however, the term is reserved for those persons for whom "been-to" has meant a long stay that has produced genuine changes and hence some serious conflicts upon the return home.
4. O. R. Dathorne, "The African Novel—Document to Experiment," *Bulletin of the Association for African Literature in English* 3 (1965): 24.
5. Cheikh Hamidou Kane, *Ambiguous Adventure* (New York: Collier Books, 1969), p. 104.
6. Ayi Kwei Armah, *Fragments* (New York: Collier Books, 1969), pp. 226–227.
7. Lillian Feder, *Ancient Myth In Modern Poetry* (Princeton: Princeton University Press, 1971), p. 11.

CHAPTER TWO

1. Mazisi Kuene, in Dennis Duerden and Cosmo Pieterse eds., *African Writers Talking* (New York: Africana Publishing Corp., 1972), p. 88.

2. From a paper read by Camara Laye at the *Colloque sur la literature africaine d'expression francaise, Faculte des Lettres de* Dakar, 26–29 March 1963, in *L'Enfant noir*, ed. Joyce A. Hutchinson (London, 1966), p. 7, and quoted in Zell and Silver, p. 151.
3. An interview by the author with Camara Laye in Dakar, 1 August, 1974.
4. Janheinz Jahn, "Discussion on Camara Laye," *Black Orpheus*, no. 6 (November 1959), p. 35, quoted in Zell and Silver, p. 151.
5. Paul Edwards and Kenneth Ramchand, "An African Sentimentalist, Camara Laye's *The Dark Child*," *African Literature Today* 4 (1970):39.
6. Ibid.
7. Camara Laye, *The Dark Child* (New York: Farrar, 1954), p. 37. Unless otherwise noted, all subsequent references to this novel will be drawn from this edition.
8. Edwards and Ramchand, pp. 39–40.
9. Ibid., p. 41.
10. Ibid., p. 40.
11. Edwards and Ramchand cite this passage from the 1955 edition of *The Dark Child* published in London by Fontana Books, p. 51.
12. Edwards and Ramchand, p. 42.
13. Ibid., pp. 42–43.
14. Ibid., p. 44.
15. D. H. Lawrence, "Why the Novel Matters," in *The Norton Anthology of English Literature*, ed. M. H. Abrams et al. (New York: Norton, 1974), 2:2148–2149.
16. Georg Lukacs, *Realism In Our Time* (New York: Harper and Row, 1971), p. 19.
17. Ernest Emenyonu, "African Literature: What Does It Take to Be Its Critic?" *African Literature Today* 5 (1971):1–11.
18. Bernth Lindfors, "Achebe's African Parable," *Presence Africaine* 66(1968): 130–136.
19. Chinua Achebe, *No Longer at Ease* (New York: Fawcett, 1969). All other references to this novel will be drawn from this edition.
20. G. D. Killam, *The Novels of Chinua Achebe* (New York: Africana Publishing Corp., 1969), p. 38.
21. Killam, p. 38.
22. Killam, who sees Obi's European morality dying with his mother, gives too little credit to African morality, too much to that of Europe, and too little to the universality of civilized acts.
23. Joseph Conrad, "Author's Note," in *Youth, A Narrative and Two Other Stories*, ed. Morton Dauwen Zabel (Garden City, New York: Doubleday, 1959), p. 29.
24. An interview by the author with Chinua Achebe at Amherst, Massachusetts, 1 May 1974. Hereafter cited in the text as "The Amherst interview."

Notes

25. Rene Wellek and Austin Warren in *Theory of Literature* (New York: Harcourt, Brace, 1949). Cite the similar journey in *Huckleberry Finn* as "a mythic plot, the meeting on the raft and journey down a great river of four who have escaped for various reasons from conventional society" (p. 224). Obi's story is informed by his having made such a journey. *No Longer at Ease* recounts the end of the journey—the attempt, doomed to fail, at reentry.
26. John Povey, "The Novels of Chinua Achebe," in *Introduction to Nigerian Literature*, ed. Bruce King (New York: Africana Publishing Corp., 1972), p. 105.
27. Adrian Roscoe, *Mother is Gold* (London: Cambridge University Press, 1971), p. 79.
28. Killam, p. 9.
29. Jacques Maquet, *Africanity* (New York: Oxford University Press, 1972), p. 68.
30. M. M. Green, *Ibo Village Affairs* (New York: Praeger, 1964), p. 158.
31. Maquet, p. 67.
32. John S. Mbiti, *African Religions and Philosophies* (Garden City, New York: Doubleday, 1970), p. 143.
33. Ibid., p. 144.
34. Lawrence, 2:2150.

CHAPTER THREE

1. Brought up on the Islamic tradition himself, Camara Laye was for a time a research fellow in Islamic Studies at Dakar University.
2. Reynolds Nicholson, *The Mystics of Islam* (London: G. Bell and Sons 1914), pp. 28–29.
3. Camara Laye, *The Radiance of the King*, trans. James Kirkup (New York: Collier Books, 1971), p. 10. All subsequent references to the novel will be drawn from this volume.
4. Nicholson, p. 37.
5. Ibid., p. 30.
6. James Olney, *Tell Me, Africa* (Princeton: Princeton University Press, 1973), p. 151.
7. Eustace Palmer, *An Introduction to the African Novel* (New York: Africana Publishing Corp., 1972), pp. 96–97, 101, 102.
8. An interview with Camara Laye by the author at Dakar, 1 August 1974. Hereafter cited in the text as "The Dakar interview."
9. Palmer, p. 96.
10. Robert Pageard, *Litterature negro-africaine* (Paris: Le livre africain, 1966), p. 87.

11. Vincent Monteil, Preface to Kane, *Ambiguous Adventure*, p. xi.
12. Katherine Woods, Foreword to Kane, *Ambiguous Adventure*, p. vii.
13. Kane, *Ambiguous Adventure*, pp. 46–47. All subsequent references to the novel are drawn from the 1969 Collier Books edition.
14. Pageard, p. 86.
15. Wilfred Cartey, Introduction to Kane, *Ambiguous Adventure*, p. xx.
16. Ibid., p. xxi.
17. Toward the end of the novel, Kane does employ the setting in France in a contentionally symbolic manner as he foreshadows the coming end of Samba Diallo's stay in Paris with a brief, late-autumn image of bare trees in a sharp wind.
18. Ibid., p. xxii.
19. Olney, p. 217.
20. Ibid., pp. 215–216.
21. Jeanne-Lydic Gore, "The Solitude of Cheikh Kane: Solitude as the Theme of 'Aventure Ambigue' by Cheikh Hamidou Kane," in *African Literature and the Universities*, ed. Gerald Moore (Ibadan: Ibadan University Press, 1965), p. 28.
22. Ibid., p. 33.
23. John Erickson, "Cheikh Hamidou Kane's *L'aventure ambigue*," an unpublished monograph presented at a conference of the African Studies Association, Syracuse, New York, 1973, p. 9.
24. Gore, p. 33.
25. Erickson, p. 13.
26. Chibli, *Vies des Saints Musulmans*, cited by Gore, p. 34, and by Moore, p. 4, in *African Literature*.
27. Moore, *African Literature*, p. 4.
28. Kane, in Moore, *African Literature*, p. 39.
29. *Ibid.*, p. 40.
30. Olney, p. 216.
31. Armah, *Fragments*. All subsequent references to the novel will be drawn from this volume.
32. Margaret Folarin, "An Additional Comment on Ayi Kwei Armah's *The Beautyful Ones Are Not Yet Born*, *African Literature Today* 5(1971):116.
33. Larson, p. 259.
34. Folarin, p. 117.
35. Ibid., p. 128.
36. Jones, review of *The Beautyful Ones Are Not Yet Born*, *African Literature Today* 3(1969):55.
37. Ibid.
38. John Povey, "The African Writer and Commitment: Ayi Kwei Armah," a monograph delivered at a conference of the African Literature Association at Austin, Texas, 1975.

39. Larson, p. 270.
40. Ibid., p. 271.
41. Melville J. Herskovitz, *The Human Factor In Changing Africa* (New York: Vintage Books, 1962), p. 102.
42. Larson, p. 271.
43. Ibid., p. 272.
44. Povey, p. 6.
45. Ibid., p. 11.
46. David I. Grossvogel, *Limits of the Novel* (Ithaca: Cornell University Press, 1968), p. 2.
47. John Patterson, *The Novel as Faith* (Boston: Gambit, 1973), p. 13.
48. Maquet, p. 65.
49. Northrop Frye, "The Archetypes of Literature," from *Kenyon Review*, Winter 1951, and from Anatomy of Criticism (Princeton: Princeton University Press, 1957), in *Myth and Method*, ed. James E. Miller, Jr. (Lincoln: University of Nebraska Press, 1960), p. 154.
50. Ibid., p. 159.
51. Maquet, p. 73.
52. Larson, p. 273n.
53. David Goldknopf, *The Life of the Novel* (Chicago: University of Chicago Press, 1972), p. 178.
54. Ibid., p. 179.
55. Povey, p. 11.
56. Ralph Freedman, *The Lyrical Novel* (Princeton: Princeton University Press, 1963), p. 198.

CHAPTER FOUR

1. Mbella Sonne Dipoko, *A Few Nights and Days* (London: Longmans, 1966), p. 4.
2. Ibid., p. 9.
3. Ayi Kwei Armah, *Why Are We So Blest?* (Garden City, New York: Doubleday, 1972), pp. 32–33.
4. Kofi Awoonor, *This Earth, My Brother* (Garden City, New York: Doubleday, 1971), p. 172. Subsequent references to the novel will be drawn from this edition.
5. Camara Laye, *A Dream of Africa*, trans. James Kirkup (New York: Collier Books, 1968), p. 25. Subsequent references to the novel will be drawn from this edition.
6. Eldred D. Jones, "Wole Soyinka's *The Interpreters*, Reading Notes," *African Literature Today* 2 (1969):42–50.

7. Eldred D. Jones, "The Essential Soyinka," in *Introduction to Nigerian Literature*, ed. Bruce King, pp. 113–132.
8. Wole Soyinka, *The Interpreters* (New York: Collier Books, 1970), p. 97. Subsequent references to the novel will be drawn from this volume.
9. Larson, p. 249.
10. Jones, "Reading Notes," p. 42–50.
11. *Ibid.*, pp. 42–43. For the narrative line of the novel, see Larson, pp. 246–254.
12. Larson, p. 254.
13. Palmer, pp. xiii–xiv.
14. Emile Snyder, Introduction to Laye, *A Dream of Africa*, p. 12.
15. Ibid., p. 17.
16. O. R. Dathorne, *The Black Mind* (Minneapolis: University of Minnesota Press, 1974), p. 377.
17. Alain Robbe-Grillet, *For a New Novel*, trans. Richard Howard (New York: Grove Press, 1965), p. 17.
18. Dathorne, *Black Mind*, p. 197.
19. Michael Echeruo, in Theophilus Vincent, ed., *The Novel and Reality in Africa and America* (Lagos: University of Lagos, Department of English and the United States Board of Foreign Scholarships, 1973), p. 25.
20. "How of my clay is made the hangman's line, Dylan Thomas," Dylan Thomas, "The force that through the green fuse drives the flower," *Collected Poems* (New York: New York Directions, 1953), p. 10.
21. Kole Omotoso in Vincent, p. 16.
22. An interview by the author with Kole Omotoso at Ibadan, Nigeria, 19 June 1974. Herafter cited in the text as "The Ibadan interview."
23. Kole Omotoso, *The Edifice* (London: Heinemann, 1971), p. 87. Subsequent references to the novel will be drawn from this volume.
24. Kole Omotoso, "New for New Horizons," 3, 5 (May 1973):43.
25. Armah, *Why Are We So Blest?* p. 71. Subsequent references to the novel will be drawn from the 1972 Doubleday edition.
26. C. G. Jung, *Man and His Symbols* (London, 1964), pp. 67 and 69, quoted in G. S. Kirk, *Myth: Its Meaning and Functions in Ancient and Other Cultures* (London: Cambridge University Press, 1970), p. 277.

CHAPTER FIVE

1. Henri Corbin, *Avicienne et le Récit Visionnaire*, Vols. 1, 2 (Paris, 1954), cited in Gore, p. 28.
2. Soyinka, "The Writer in a Modern African State," in *The Writer In Modern*

Notes

Africa, ed. Per Wastberg (New York: Africana Publishing Corp., 1969), p. 17.

3. Soyinka, *Season of Anomy* (New York: Third Press, 1974), p. 56. *Season of Anomy* is the latest work of what Soyinka has called his War Quartet. The other works include *A Shuttle in the Crypt*, a collection of poems; *Madmen and Specialists*, a play; and *The Man Died*, taken from Soyinka's diaries kept during his two-year imprisonment during Nigeria's civil war.

4. Kole Omotoso, "Politics, Propaganda, and Prostitution," *Afriscope* 4, 11 (November 1974):47.

5. Ayi Kwei Armah, *Two Thousand Seasons* (Nairobi: East African Publishing House, 1973), pp. 313–314.

6. John Grimond, "Africa: The Agony of Western Ways," *New York Times*, 22 December 1974, section E, p. 7.

7. Ibid.

8. Feder, p. 5.

9. Bernth Lindfors, "Critical Approaches to Folklore in African Literature," in *African Folklore*, ed. Richard Dorson (New York: Anchor Books, 1972), p. 4.

10. Maquet, p. 73.

Works Cited

Achebe, Chinua. *No Longer at Ease*. New York: Fawcett World Library, 1969.

Aidoo, Amm Atta. "Everything Counts." *No Sweetness Here*. New York: Anchor Books, 1972.

Aluko, T. M. *Kinsman and Foreman*. London: Heinemann Educational Books, 1966.

Armah, Ayi Kwei. *The Beautyful Ones Are Not Yet Born*. New York: Collier Books, 1968.

————. *Fragments*. New York: Collier Books, 1969.

————. *Two Thousand Seasons*. Nairobi: East Africa Publishing House, 1973.

————. *Why Are We So Blest?* Garden City, New York: Doubleday and Co., 1972.

Awoonor, Kofi. *This Earth, My Brother*. Garden City, New York: Doubleday and Co., 1971.

Conrad, Joseph. *Youth*, edited by Morton Dauwen Zabel. Garden City, New York: Doubleday and Co., 1949.

Dathorne, O. R. *"The African Novel—Document to Experiment."* *Bulletin of the Association for African Literature in English* 3 (1965): 18–39.

————. *The Black Mind*. Minneapolis: University of Minnesota Press, 1974.

Dipoko, Mbella Sonne. *A Few Nights and Days*. London: Longmans, Green, and Co., 1966.

Duerden, Dennis, and Cosmo Pieterse, eds. *African Writers Talking*. New York: Africana Publishing Corp., 1972.

Edwards, Paul, and Kenneth Ramchand. "An African Sentimentalist, Camara Laye's *The Dark Child*." *African Literature Today* 4 (1970): 37–53.

Emenyonu, Ernest. "African Literature: What Does it Take to be its Critic?" *African Literature Today* 5 (1971):1–11.

Erickson, John. "Cheikh Hamidou Kane's *L'aventure ambigue*." An unpublished monograph delivered at a meeting of the African Studies Association at Syracuse, New York, 1973.

Feder, Lillian. *Ancient Myth in Modern Poetry*. Princeton: Princeton University Press, 1971.

Folarin, Margaret. "An Additional Comment on Ayi Kwei Armah's *The Beautyful Ones Are Not Yet Born*." *African Literature Today* 5 (1971):116–128.

Freedman, Ralph. *The Lyrical Novel*. Princeton: Princeton University Press, 1963.

Frye, Northrop. "The Archetypes in Literature." In *Myth and Method*, edited by James E. Miller, Jr. Lincoln: University of Nebraska Press, 1960.

Goldknopf, David. *The Life of the Novel*. Chicago: University of Chicago Press, 1972.

Gore, Jeanne-Lydic. "The Solitude of Cheikh Kane: Solitude as the Theme of 'Aventure Ambigue' by Cheikh Hamidou Kane." In African Literature and the Universities, edited by Gerald Moore. Ibadan: Ibadan University Press, 1965.

Green, M. M. *Ibo Village Affairs*. New York: Frederick A. Praeger, 1964.

Grimond, John. "Africa: The Agony of Western Ways." *New York Times*, 22 December 1974, section E, p. 7.

Grossvogel, David I. *Limits of the Novel*. Ithaca: Cornell University Press, 1968.

Herskovitz, Melville J. *The Human Factor in Changing Africa*. New York: Vintage Books, 1962.

Ifejika, Samuel. "The Malaise of Youth." In *Insider*. Enugu, Nigeria: Nwanko-Ifejika and Co., 1971, pp. 51–72.

Jones, Eldred D. Review of *The Beautyful Ones Are Not Yet Born*. *African Literature Today* 3 (1969):55–57.

———. "The Essential Soyinka." In *Introduction to Nigerian Literature*, edited by Bruce King. New York: Africana Publishing Corp., 1972.

———. "Wole Soyinka's *The Interpreters*, Reading Notes." *African Literature Today* 2 (1969):42–50.

Kane, Cheikh Hamidou. *Ambiguous Adventure*. Trans. Katherine Woods. New York: Collier Books, 1969.

Killam, G. D. *The Novels of Chinua Achebe*. New York: Africana Publishing Corporation, 1969.

Works Cited

King, Bruce. ed. *Introduction to Nigerian Literature*. New York: Africana Publishing Corporation, 1972.

Kirk, G. S. *Myth: Its Meaning and Functions in Ancient and Other Cultures*. London: Cambridge University Press, 1970.

Larson, Charles R. *The Emergence of African Fiction*. Bloomington: Indiana University Press, 1971.

Lawrence, D. H. "Why the Novel Matters." In *The Norton Anthology of English Literature*, edited by M. H. Abrams, et al. 3rd ed. 2 vols. New York: W. W. Norton and Co., 1974.

Laye, Camara. *The Dark Child*. Trans. James Kirkup and Ernest Jones. New York: Farrar, Straus and Giroux, 1954.

―――. *A Dream of Africa*. Trans. James Kirkup. New York: Collier Books, 1968.

―――. *The Radiance of the King*. Trans. James Kirkup. New York: Collier Books, 1971.

Lindfors, Bernth. "Achebe's African Parable." *Presence Africaine* 66 (1968):130–136.

―――. "Critical Approaches to Folklore in African Literature." In *African Folklore*, edited by Richard Corson. New York: Anchor Books, 1972.

Lukacs, Georg. *Realism in Our Time*. New York: Harper and Row, 1971.

Maquet, Jacques. *Africanity: The Cultural Unity of Black Africa*. Trans. Joan R. Rayfield. New York: Oxford University Press, 1972.

Mbiti, John S. *African Religions and Philosophies*. Garden City, New York: Doubleday and Co., 1970.

Nicholson, Reynolds. *The Mystics of Islam*. London: G. Bell and Sons, 1914.

Okara, Gabriel. *The Voice*. London: Andre Deutsch, 1964.

Olney, James. *Tell Me, Africa*. Princeton: Princeton University Press, 1973.

Omotoso, Kole. *The Edifice*. London: Heinemann, Educational Books, 1971.

―――. "New For New Horizons." *Afriscope* 3, no. 5 (May 1973): 43–45.

―――. "Politics, Propaganda, and Prostitution." *Afriscope* 4, no. 11 (November 1974):47–49.

Pageard, Robert. *Littérature négro-africaine*. Paris: Le Livre africaine, 1966.

Palmer, Eustace. *An Introduction to the African Novel*. New York: Africana Publishing Corp., 1972.

Patterson, John. *The Novel as Faith*. Boston: Gambit, 1973.

Povey, John. "The African Writer and Commitment: Ayi Kwei Armah." A paper delivered at a conference of the African Literature Association at Austin, Texas, 1975.

————. "The Novels of Chinua Achebe." In *Introduction to Nigerian Literature*, edited by Bruce King. New York: Africana Publishing Corp., 1972.

Robbe-Grillet, Alain. *For a New Novel*. Trans. Richard Howard. New York: Grove Press, 1965.

Roscoe, Adrian A. *Mother is Gold: A Study In West African Fiction*. London: Cambridge University Press, 1971.

Soyinka, Wole. *The Interpreters*. New York: Collier Books, 1970.

————. *Season of Anomy*. New York: Third Press, 1974.

————. "The Writer In a Modern African State." In *The Writer in Modern Africa*, edited by Per Wastberg. New York: Africana Publishing Corp., 1969.

Vincent, Theophilus, ed. *The Novel and Reality in Africa and America*. Lagos: University of Lagos, Department of English and the United States Board of Foreign Scholarships, 1973.

Wellek, René, and Warren, Austin. *Theory of Literature*. New York: Harcourt, Brace and Co., 1949.

Zell, Hans, and Silver, Helene. *A Reader's Guide to African Literature*. New York: Africana Publishing Corp., 1971.

Index

abortion, 40–42

Achebe, Chinua, 20, 24, 28, 37, 38, 42, 71; on Armah, 85–86. Works: *Arrow of God*, 21, 33; *No Longer at Ease*, 5, 6, 12, 19–43, 71, 90, 127, 131, 135n.25; *A Man of the People*, 21; *Things Fall Apart*, 20, 21, 31. *See also* character studies

Africa, internal issues of, 127–128; life in French West, 15–18; self-development of, 108. *See also* New Africa

Africa, the West and, 7, 62, 64, 69–70, 85, 108, 110–111, 120, 128. *See also* been-to; conflict

Africa, Westernization destructive to, 3, 54, 60, 87, 120, 123

African literature: growth of, 1–2, 113, 130–131; future of novel in, 87. *See also* novels, West African novelists

afterlife, 59, 68, 83–84. *See also* spirit world

Aidoo, Amma Atta, 90

Alice in Wonderland, 47

alienation, of been-to, 16, 22, 71, 79, 92. *See also* been-to; corruption, isolation

Aluko, T. M., 90–91

Ambiguous Adventure. *See* Kane, Cheikh Hamidou

Ancient Myth and Modern Poetry, 8

archetype, 124

Armah, Ayi Kwei: disengagement of feeling for home country, 85–86. Works: *The Beautyful Ones Are Not Yet Born*, 72, 74, 84–85, 86, 106, 120; *Fragments*, 6, 70, 89, 93, 95, 109, 120, 127, 131; (compared with *Ambiguous Adventure*) 70; *Two Thousand Seasons*, 128; *Why Are We So Blest?* 7, 90, 112–124, 129. *See also* character studies

Awoonor, Kofi. Work: *This Earth, My Brother*, 90, 104–108, 127. *See also* character studies

been-to: adjustments of, 3; as embodiment of Africa, 82; changing attitudes toward, 4; castigation of; 112; changes in meaning of phrase; 133 n.3; as character in West African novels, 1–9, 11–43, 45–131; conscience of, 55, 69; culture shock of, 128–129; definition of, 2; disaster for, 93; dual identities of, 12, 61; emotional disturbance of, 78, 79;

Index

heterodoxy, 24
host, responsibility of: as powerful social imperative in African cultures, 27
Huckleberry Finn, 135 n.25
hubris, 82

Ibo, the, 21, 31–32; been-to novel as cautionary tale of, 19–43; *osu* in society of, 38
independence: of African nations, 1, 21; cultural, 123
indigenous stranger. *See* been-to
individualism vs. communalism, 23, 26. *See also* communalism
individualism, Western, 38
individualist in Africa, 11–12
Inferno, 107
initiation: Konden Diara as, 15, 18; Yondo as, 129, 130
The Interpreters. See Soyinka, Wole
Islam, 100; beliefs of, 60–61; culture of, 13; influence of in novels, 54; mystical awareness in, 126; spirituality in, 59; tradition of, 135 n.1; values of, 48; water world of spirituality in, 68. *See also* conflict
isolation, 3, 73, 77–78, 93, 127, 131. *See also* alienation, been-to

Jahn, Janheinz, 15
Jones, Eldred, 96, 97
journey. *See* traveler
"Journey of the Magi," 21
Joycean posture, of been-tos, 93
Jung, Carl, 124

Kafka, Franz, 52
Kane, Cheikh Hamidou, 55, 71, 86, 87. Work: *Ambiguous Adventure*, 6, 53–70, 71, 73–74, 87, 89, 126, 131 (compared to *The Radiance of the King*) 54. *See also* character studies

Karim, 1
Kierkegaard, Sören, 107
Kinsman and Foreman, 90–91
kola nut. *See* sacrifice
Konden Diara. *See initiation*
Koran. See Word of Koran

Lagos, 19, 24–25, 26, 29, 30
Landscape. *See* novel, setting of
Larson, Charles R., 97
Lawrence, D. H., 19–20, 43
Laye, Camara, 72, 86, 87; Islamic studies of, 135 n.1; life of compared to Kane, 55. Works: *The Dark Child*, 5, 12–19, 99, 102, 103, 104, 126; *A Dream of Africa*, 6, 12, 90, 91, 93, 98–104 (flaws in) 101–104; *The Radiance of the King*, 5–6, 12, 13, 45, 46–54, 87, 102, 103, 104, 131. *See also* character studies
The Life of the Novel, 86
Lindfors, Bernth, 21, 130
literature. *See* African literature; novels; West African novelists
logos, 22, 35
Lukács, Georg, 20, 30, 33

magic, 11, 17, 18
marriage, 38–42. *See also* polygamy
Maquet, Jacques, 131
materialism, 74, 80. *See also* been-to; character studies (Brempong)
metamorphosis, 8, 14, 28, 125, 130
Mofolo, Thomas, 1
Moore, Gerald, 68
morality, 134 n.22
mourning. *See* disorder
mutability in modern Africa, 14, 131
mysticism, African Islamic, 45, 126. *See also* Islam
myth, 6, 8–9, 45, 118
myth, of the water goddess, 85
mythic figures, visions of, 87

148

religion, traditional: declining power
of, 76
return, in West African novel, 2, 19,
70–72, 73, 74, 76–77, 99. *See also*
been-to; conflict, individual; reassimilation; traveler
revolution, 116, 117, 120
ritual, 11, 85. *See also* initiation
ritual: death of been-to as, 112–124;
jewelry making as, 16–17; Night of
the Koran as, 65; Obi's journey as,
32; "outdooring" as, 79; relationship of to myth, 84, 129
ritualistic properties, of been-to, 9
Robbe-Grillet, Alain, 103
Roscoe, Adrian, 36

sacrifice, of kola nut, 32, 34–35
science, as solution, 61, 63
Senegal, 1, 6
Sesuto, 1
sexual hunger, 120, 121, 122–123
Snyder, Emile, 99
Socé, Ousman, 1
social consciousness, in African tradition, 84–85
social criticism, in been-to novel, 91,
111
social disaster. *See* Guinea
social disorder, *See* disorder
social realism, 29, 70, 81, 83
social reality in contemporary Africa,
21–22, 86, 87, 93, 106, 107
society, dangers of: to been-to, 92
society, traditional in Africa, 22–23.
See also culture
Soyinka, Wole, 126, 139 n.3. Works:
The Interpreters, 6, 90, 91, 94–98,
127 (flaws in) 96–97, 98; *Season of
Anomy*, 127, 130, 139 n.3. *See also*
character studies
spirit, communication with, 39

spirituality, 55, 61, 62, 64
spirit world, 32, 33–35, 39–40, 72, 82;
West as, 34, 37–38, 81; "wrestling
in the," 32, 42, 45, 71. *See also*
afterlife
Sufi Path, 46–54
"Swiftian preoccupation," 72, 75
symbolism, 103, 105, 123
syncretism, 60, 63
synthesis, 70, 85

This Earth, My Brother. *See* Awoonor,
Kofi
Thomas, Dylan, 106
traumatization, private: in confrontation with African and Western cultures, 12, 14, 20
traveler: journey of, 135 n.25; as literary convention, 42; on metaphorical journey, 71; to West, 11–12; to
world of other spirits, 83. *See also*
been-to; division, personal; reassimilation; return
The Traveller of the East, 1

The Voice, 91

The Waste Land, 3, 106, 107
West. *See* Africa, West and; Africa,
Westernization of
West African novelists. *See* separate
entries for Achebe, Chinua; Armah,
Ayi Kwei; Awoonor, Kofi; Kane,
Cheikh Hamidou; Laye, Camara;
Omotoso, Kole; Soyinka, Wole. *See
also* African literature; novels
Western civilization, attack on. *See*
harvest, rice
Western scar, 3, 64, 66, 94; healing of,
104; Armah's view of, 112
white race, destructive forces of, 115,
118

Index

Why Are We So Blest? *See* Armah, Ayi
  Kwei
Woods, Katherine, 55
Word of Koran, 65, 66

young man from the provinces, 4
youth of promise, 24, 30
Yondo. *See* initiation
Yoruba, 109